THE SECRET TO
PERSONAL
BRANDING
POWER

BOOKS FOR TODAY'S LIFESTYLE; BE A PART OF THE JOURNEY

THE SECRET TO PERSONAL BRANDING POWER

CONTENTS

INTRODUCTION

Imagine having the power to create an indelible impression on people's minds, inspiring them to trust and follow you. Imagine being the go-to person in your field, able to command respect, influence others, and achieve your goals. This is the power of personal branding and the secret to success in today's fast-paced and competitive business world.

Whether you're a budding entrepreneur, a seasoned professional, or someone looking to advance your career, personal branding can help you stand out and achieve your goals. It's not just about having a great resume or a flashy website; it's about building an authentic, memorable, and compelling brand that resonates with your target audience.

In this Book, we will explore the art and science of personal branding, uncovering the secrets to creating a powerful brand that reflects your unique personality, values, and goals. We will delve into the psychology of branding, understanding what motivates people to choose one brand over another and how you can leverage these insights to build a strong and enduring brand.

From defining your brand identity to crafting a killer elevator pitch and leveraging social media to creating a personal brand strategy, this Book will provide you with the tools, insights, and inspiration you need to build a personal brand that commands attention, respect, and admiration.

Whether you're a freelancer, a consultant, a job seeker, or an entrepreneur, the secret to personal branding power is within your reach. With the right mindset, strategy, and tactics, you can create a brand that speaks to your strengths, resonates with your audience, and propels you toward success. So, let's get started on this exciting journey to personal branding excellence!

CHAPTER 1
THE BASICS OF PERSONAL BRANDING

Are you looking to stand out in your industry, differentiate yourself from your competition, and become recognized as a leader in your field? Then personal branding is the key to achieving these goals. A great skillset or product is not enough in the current business world. You must showcase your unique strengths, personality, and values to attract and retain customers, partners, and employers.

That's where the basics of personal branding come in. In this chapter, we'll cover the foundational principles of personal branding and provide actionable tips and strategies to create a powerful brand that aligns with your goals and resonates with your target audience. From defining your brand identity and messaging to building your online presence and leveraging your network, you'll learn how to take control of your personal brand and unleash your full potential. Let's dive in!

Personal Branding

Personal branding has become more important than ever as the world becomes increasingly digital. In today's fast-paced society, it's not enough to simply have a good reputation - you need to be able to showcase your unique value proposition to stand out from the crowd.

Personal branding is about creating a unique identity that reflects your personality, values, and expertise. It's about establishing yourself as an authority in your field and making a positive impression on the people you interact with.

One of the most important aspects of personal branding is consistency. Your brand should be consistent across all platforms, from social media profiles to business cards. This means using the same colors, fonts, and messaging to ensure that people recognize your brand wherever they see it.

Another important aspect of personal branding is authenticity. Your brand should reflect who you are, not just what you do. If you try to create a brand that isn't authentic, people will see through it, and you'll lose credibility.

To create an effective personal brand, you need to clearly understand your unique value proposition. This means identifying what sets you apart from your competition and what you can offer that no one else can. Once you've identified your unique value proposition, you can use it to create a messaging strategy that communicates your brand effectively.

Your messaging strategy should be focused on your target audience. You need to understand your audience, their needs, and how you can help them. This means creating content that speaks directly to your audience and providing value through your expertise.

Social media is a powerful tool for personal branding. It lets you connect with people worldwide and showcase your expertise to a wider audience. However, it's important to use social media strategically. You need to choose the platforms most relevant to your brand and your target audience and use them consistently to build your brand.

Personal branding is not just about promoting yourself; it's also about building relationships with others. Networking is a key component of personal branding, as it allows you to connect with people who can help you achieve your goals. Whether attending industry events, joining online communities, or reaching out to potential collaborators, networking can help you expand your reach and build valuable connections that benefit you in the long run.

Another important aspect of personal branding is telling your story effectively. Your story sets you apart from others and helps people connect with you on a deeper level. It's important to communicate your story compellingly, whether through your website, social media profiles, or in-person interactions. Sharing your story can create a strong emotional connection with your audience and build a more powerful personal brand.

Finally, personal branding is not just about promoting yourself; it's also about giving back to your community. Whether through volunteering, mentorship, or charitable donations, finding ways to give back can help you establish yourself as a leader and a positive influence in your industry. By demonstrating your commitment to making a difference, you can build a personal brand that reflects your expertise, values, and desire to make a positive impact in the world.

Finally, personal branding is an ongoing process. It's not something you can do once and forget about - you need to constantly work on building and improving your brand. This means staying up-to-date with the latest trends and technologies and continually refining your messaging strategy to stay relevant and impactful.

Power Branding

Personal branding has become a buzzword in recent years, with individuals and businesses alike recognizing the value of creating a strong brand identity. But what sets apart a successful personal brand from an average one? The answer lies in the concept of power branding.

Power branding is the process of creating a personal brand that not only represents who you are but also has the ability to influence others and drive action. It is about creating a brand that resonates with your audience and establishes you as an authority in your field. So, how can you create a powerful personal brand? Here are some key strategies to keep in mind:

1. Define your brand identity

The first step to creating a powerful personal brand is to define your brand identity. This involves identifying your unique strengths, values, and personality traits that set you apart from others. Take the time to reflect on your experiences, skills, and passions to determine what makes you unique.

Once you have a clear understanding of your brand identity, you can start to develop a brand strategy that aligns with your goals and values. This includes creating a consistent brand voice, visual identity, and messaging that accurately represents who you are and what you stand for.

2. Establish your authority

Power branding is all about establishing yourself as an authority in your field. This requires building credibility through a variety of channels, such as publishing content, speaking at events, and engaging with your audience on social media.

By sharing your expertise and insights, you can position yourself as a thought leader in your industry and gain the trust and respect of your audience. This, in turn, can help you build a loyal following and drive action around your brand.

3. Leverage your network

Building a powerful personal brand requires more than just individual effort - it also involves leveraging your network to expand your reach and influence. This means engaging with other thought leaders in your industry, collaborating on projects, and seeking out opportunities to connect with new audiences.

By building strong relationships with others in your industry, you can tap into new audiences and amplify your message. This can also help you stay up-to-date on the latest trends and developments in your field, which can be invaluable for staying ahead of the competition.

4. Consistency is key

One of the most important elements of power branding is consistency. This means maintaining a consistent brand voice, visual identity, and messaging across all channels and touchpoints. This helps to reinforce your brand identity and establish a strong, recognizable presence in the minds of your audience.

Consistency also helps to build trust and credibility with your audience, as it shows that you are reliable and dependable. By staying true to your brand identity and values, you can create a powerful personal brand that resonates with your audience and drives action.

5. Be Authentic

Authenticity is one of the key pillars of power branding. It is essential to be true to yourself and stay authentic in all your interactions with your audience. When building your personal brand, it is important to avoid presenting a false image of yourself that is not in line with your values, personality, or beliefs. Your audience can quickly detect when you are being inauthentic, which can harm your brand reputation. Always remember to stay true to yourself, and let your brand reflect who you are as a person.

6. Tell Your Story

Storytelling is a powerful tool for building a personal brand. By sharing your personal story, you can create an emotional connection with your audience and build trust. Your story can also help you differentiate yourself from others in your industry and make you more relatable to your audience. Be creative in your storytelling and find ways to convey your experiences and values in a way that resonates with your audience.

7. Monitor Your Reputation

As your personal brand grows, it becomes increasingly important to monitor your reputation online. This means regularly checking your social media profiles, search engine results, and other online channels to ensure that your brand is being portrayed in a positive light. Negative comments or feedback can harm your brand reputation, so it is essential to address any issues promptly and professionally. You can also use online reputation management tools to monitor your brand reputation and take proactive steps to protect it.

8. Stay Relevant

Finally, it is important to stay relevant in your industry and adapt to changing trends and developments. This means staying up-to-date on the latest news and developments in your field and constantly evolving your brand strategy to keep pace with changing market conditions. By staying relevant, you can maintain your position as a thought leader in your industry and continue to drive success for your personal brand.

The Power of Branding

Have you ever wondered why some brands are more popular than others? How can certain companies charge a premium price for a product or service while others struggle to compete on price alone? The answer lies in the power of branding. Branding is the process of creating a unique image and name for a product, service, or person. It is what sets you apart from the competition and helps you to stand out in a crowded market.

When it comes to personal branding, the same principles apply. You are your own brand, and your unique image and reputation can help you to achieve your goals, whether that's finding a new job, building a successful business, or becoming an influencer in your industry. By creating a strong personal brand, you can establish yourself as an authority in your field and build trust with your audience.

One of the key benefits of personal branding is that it can help you to attract the right opportunities. When you have a clear and consistent brand message, you are more likely to attract the attention of potential clients, employers, and collaborators who share your values and vision. By building a strong personal brand, you can also increase your visibility and credibility in your industry, which can lead to more speaking engagements, media opportunities, and partnerships.

Another powerful aspect of branding is the emotional connection it can create with your audience. People don't just buy products or services; they buy experiences and emotions. A strong brand can tap into the emotions and values of your audience, creating a deeper connection that goes beyond the functional benefits of what you offer. By crafting a clear and compelling brand story, you can create a sense of purpose and meaning for your audience, which can lead to long-term loyalty and advocacy.

But creating a strong personal brand is not just about having a fancy logo or a catchy slogan. It requires a deep understanding of who you are, what you stand for, and what makes you unique. Your personal brand should reflect your values, personality, and expertise, and it should be authentic and consistent across all your communication channels. This means that your website, social media profiles, and other marketing materials should all convey the same message and tone and should be aligned with your overall brand strategy.

In addition, personal branding requires ongoing effort and investment. Building a strong personal brand is a long-term process, and it requires consistent messaging, engagement, and evaluation. You need to constantly assess your brand image and reputation, listen to feedback from your audience, and adapt your strategy as needed. This means that personal branding is not a one-time project but a continuous journey of self-discovery and growth.

In conclusion, the power of branding cannot be underestimated when it comes to personal branding. A strong personal brand can help you to achieve your goals, attract the right opportunities, create emotional connections with your audience, and establish yourself as an authority in your field. However, building a strong personal brand requires a deep understanding of who you are, what you stand for, and what makes you unique, as well as ongoing effort and investment. By investing in your personal brand, you can create a lasting legacy that reflects your values, passions, and expertise and that helps you to achieve your full potential.

The What, Why, and How of Personal Branding (Everything You Need To Know)

Personal branding is the process of creating and managing your unique identity, image, and reputation in the public sphere. It involves using your strengths, values, and personality to build a distinct brand that stands out in your industry or niche.

Why is Personal Branding Important?

Personal branding is essential in today's highly competitive world. It helps you differentiate yourself from others and showcase your unique value proposition. A strong personal brand can help you:

1. Build credibility and trust - When people know who you are, what you stand for, and what you offer, they are more likely to trust you and do business with you.

2. Create opportunities - A strong personal brand can help you attract new clients, job offers, speaking engagements, and other exciting opportunities.

3. Establish expertise - By sharing your knowledge, opinions, and insights on your area of expertise, you can establish yourself as a thought leader in your field.

4. Stand out in a crowded market - In a world where everyone is trying to get noticed, a strong personal brand can help you rise above the noise and stand out in your industry.

5. Enhance your personal reputation - A strong personal brand can enhance your reputation and make you more credible and trustworthy in the eyes of your audience.

6. Increase your market value - A well-known personal brand can increase your market value, making it easier to negotiate higher salaries, fees, and rates.

7. Build a community of supporters - A strong personal brand can help you build a community of supporters who believe in you and your vision. These supporters

can become advocates for your brand and help you grow your business or career.

8. Boost your self-confidence - A well-defined personal brand can boost your self-confidence and give you a sense of purpose and direction.

9. Stand out in job applications - A strong personal brand can help you stand out in job applications and differentiate yourself from other candidates.

10. Create a legacy - A strong personal brand can create a legacy that lasts beyond your lifetime. By sharing your knowledge and insights, you can inspire others and leave a lasting impact on your industry or community.

11. Foster creativity and innovation - Building a personal brand requires creativity and innovation, which can help you develop new ideas and approaches in your work and life.

How to Build Your Personal Brand

Building your personal brand takes time and effort, but it is worth it. Here are the steps you can take to build your personal brand:

1. Define your brand identity - Start by identifying your strengths, values, and personality traits that make you unique. Think about what you want to be known for and what you stand for.

2. Develop your brand message - Your brand message should communicate who you are, what you do, and what sets you apart from others in your field. It should

be clear, concise, and consistent across all your communication channels.

3. Build your online presence - In today's digital age, your online presence is critical to your personal brand. Create a professional website, social media profiles, and other online platforms to showcase your brand and connect with your audience.

4. Share your expertise - Share your knowledge, opinions, and insights on your area of expertise through blog posts, articles, videos, podcasts, and other content formats. This will help you establish yourself as a thought leader in your field.

5. Monitor and manage your brand - Keep track of what people are saying about you online and respond to feedback in a professional and timely manner. Regularly review and update your brand message and online presence to stay relevant and competitive.

6. Create valuable content - To attract and retain your audience, create content that provides value to them. Your content can be in the form of blog posts, articles, videos, podcasts, infographics, or any other format that resonates with your audience. Make sure that your content is informative, engaging, and relevant to your niche.

7. Use SEO - Use search engine optimization (SEO) techniques to make your content visible to your target audience. Research keywords that your audience is searching for, and use them in your content, titles, meta descriptions, and other areas to increase your visibility and reach.

8. Develop a personal style - Develop a personal style that reflects your brand identity and resonates with your audience. Your style can include your tone of voice, visual identity, branding elements, and other factors that make your brand unique and memorable.

9. Collaborate with others - Collaborate with other professionals, influencers, or brands in your industry. This can help you expand your reach, attract new audiences, and build relationships with other professionals.

10. Engage in social media - Use social media platforms to engage with your audience, share your content, and showcase your brand. Identify the platforms that your audience uses the most and create a consistent presence there.

11. Attend events - Attend industry events, conferences, or meetups to network with other professionals and learn from experts in your field. This can help you expand your knowledge, make new connections, and build your brand.

12. Get feedback and adjust - Regularly review your brand message, online presence, and content to see what works and what doesn't. Use feedback from your audience, clients, or peers to adjust your brand accordingly and improve your performance.

CHAPTER 2

BUSINESS/PROFESSIONAL BRANDING

When it comes to personal branding, establishing a strong business/professional brand is crucial for standing out in a competitive market. A well-defined business/professional brand can help you establish credibility, attract clients, and create a clear direction for your career.

In this chapter of "The Secret to Personal Branding Power," we will delve into the nuances of business/professional branding, from defining your unique value proposition to creating a consistent brand image across all your marketing channels. We will also explore how to use social media and other online platforms to build your brand and reach a wider audience.

With the right strategies and tools, you can build a powerful business/professional brand that not only helps you achieve your career goals but also helps you make a meaningful impact on your industry. So, let's get started and discover the secrets to personal branding power!

Personal and Corporate Success through Branding

In today's competitive market, personal branding is essential to creating a unique and recognizable identity in the business world. A well-defined brand strategy can help individuals and companies stand out from the crowd, increase their visibility, and attract more customers or clients. In this section, we will explore the ways in which personal and corporate branding can lead to success.

Firstly, personal branding is crucial for professionals who want to establish themselves as experts in their field. By creating a unique personal brand, individuals can differentiate themselves from their peers, demonstrate their expertise and knowledge, and showcase their values and beliefs. This can lead to increased opportunities for networking, speaking engagements, and career advancement.

Moreover, a strong personal brand can also lead to increased credibility and trust. Clients and customers are more likely to do business with individuals who have a clear and consistent personal brand. A well-defined personal brand can also help to build stronger relationships with clients or customers, as they feel more connected to the individual behind the brand.

Similarly, corporate branding is essential for businesses looking to differentiate themselves from their competitors. A strong corporate brand can help companies establish themselves as leaders in their industry, build brand loyalty among customers, and attract top talent. A well-defined brand strategy can also help to create a consistent and recognizable image across all marketing channels, including social media, websites, and advertising.

Moreover, a strong corporate brand can lead to increased customer loyalty and retention. Customers are more likely to continue doing business with companies that have a strong and consistent brand identity. A strong brand can also help to create a sense of community among customers, who feel connected to the company and its values.

Furthermore, corporate branding can also lead to increased employee satisfaction and retention. Employees who feel connected to the company's brand and values are more likely to be engaged and committed to their work. A strong brand can also help to attract top talent, as job candidates are more likely to be attracted to companies with a clear and consistent brand identity.

In order to create a successful personal or corporate brand, it is essential to have a clear understanding of the target audience. This involves identifying the needs, desires, and values of the audience, as well as their preferences for communication channels and styles. Once the target audience has been identified, it is important to develop a unique and authentic brand identity that resonates with them.

Moreover, a successful brand strategy should be consistent across all marketing channels, including social media, websites, and advertising. This includes using consistent branding elements such as colors, logos, and messaging. Consistency is key to creating a recognizable and memorable brand identity.

In addition to establishing a clear brand identity, it is also important to consistently communicate the brand message. This involves developing a consistent tone of voice and messaging that aligns with the brand identity. By consistently communicating the brand message across all marketing channels, individuals and companies can create a strong brand perception among their target audience.

Furthermore, personal and corporate branding can also help to create a sense of purpose and direction. By defining a clear brand identity, individuals and companies can establish values and beliefs that guide their decision-making and actions. This can help create a sense of purpose and direction, which can motivate both individuals and teams.

Finally, a strong brand can also lead to increased profitability. Customers are often willing to pay a premium for products or services from companies with a strong and recognizable brand identity. Additionally, a strong brand can help create a competitive advantage, making it more difficult for competitors to replicate the same brand recognition and loyalty.

The truth is personal and corporate branding is an essential component of success in today's business world. By establishing a unique and consistent brand identity, individuals and companies can differentiate themselves from their competitors, attract new customers or clients, and build brand loyalty. A strong brand can also increase credibility and trust, employee satisfaction and retention, and profitability. To succeed in today's competitive market, individuals and companies must prioritize developing and maintaining a strong and authentic brand identity.

How the Corporate Giants Prospered through Branding

The world's leading corporate giants have prospered through effective branding strategies, enabling them to establish themselves as household names and dominate their respective industries.

One of the best examples of successful branding is Apple Inc. Apple's success story perfectly shows how branding can change the game. Apple has been able to create a cult-like following by creating a brand that is synonymous with innovation, creativity, and quality. Apple's brand is so strong that its products are highly anticipated, and customers will camp outside stores to get their hands on the latest iPhone or iPad.

Another great example of branding success is Nike. Nike has been able to create a brand that is associated with performance, style, and success. Their "Just Do It" slogan has become an iconic phrase that inspires athletes worldwide to push their limits and achieve their goals. Nike's brand is so strong that even those not interested in sports or athletics still recognize the brand and the logo.

The success of these companies and many others can be attributed to their ability to create a strong brand identity that resonates with their target audience. They have created a unique brand identity that sets them apart from their competitors and makes them instantly recognizable to consumers.

One of the key elements of successful branding is consistency. Corporate giants have consistently maintained their brand identity and messaging across all platforms. From the packaging of their products to the design of their websites, every element of their branding is consistent and reinforces their brand identity.

Another crucial aspect of branding success is understanding your target audience. Corporate giants deeply understand their target audience's wants, needs, and aspirations, enabling them to create products and services that resonate with their customers.

Brand messaging is another essential element of branding success. Corporate giants have been able to create a clear and concise brand message that communicates their value proposition to their customers. They have communicated their brand message effectively across all platforms, which has helped establish them as leaders in their respective industries.

Case Studies: Five Businesses that Failed Due to Poor or Bad Branding

Business branding is a crucial aspect of any successful venture. A brand is an image that the public has of your company, and it is essential to cultivate a positive reputation. This section will look at five failed businesses due to poor or bad branding.

1. Blockbuster

Blockbuster was a dominant force in the video rental market in the 1990s. However, the company failed to anticipate the impact of streaming services, such as Netflix. Instead of adapting to the changing market, Blockbuster continued with its outdated business model. It did not help that the company's brand was associated with high and late rental fees. Blockbuster eventually filed for bankruptcy in 2010.

Blockbuster was once the go-to destination for movie rentals, with thousands of stores across the United States. However, the rise of digital streaming services in the late 2000s, such as Netflix and Hulu, made it increasingly difficult for Blockbuster to remain competitive. The company attempted to adapt by introducing its online rental service, but it was too late. The Blockbuster brand became synonymous with outdated technology and high rental fees, driving customers away in droves.

One of the major factors that contributed to Blockbuster's downfall was its lack of foresight. The company failed to anticipate the impact that digital streaming would have on the industry and was slow to adapt to the changing landscape. In contrast, Netflix recognized the potential of online streaming early on and invested heavily in the technology. This allowed Netflix to gain a significant market share and eventually overtake Blockbuster as the leading movie rental service.

Another issue that plagued Blockbuster was its complicated fee structure. The company charged customers late fees for returning movies past the due date, a widely criticized practice for being excessive and unfair. In addition, the fees for renting movies were often higher than those of its competitors, further damaging the Blockbuster brand. As a result, customers began seeking alternatives, such as Redbox, which offered cheaper rental fees and a more convenient rental process.

2. Kodak

Kodak was once a household name in the photography industry. However, the company failed to keep up with the times. Kodak was slow to embrace digital photography and continued to focus on film. The company's brand became associated with outdated technology, and it lost its market share to companies like Canon and Nikon.

Kodak's brand was built on the premise of film photography, and the company enjoyed a significant market share in the film and camera industry. However, the rise of digital photography significantly changed the industry. Kodak was slow to adapt to the new technology and failed to realize the potential of digital photography. The company's brand was associated with outdated technology and struggled to compete with new entrants like Canon and Nikon. Despite trying to enter the digital market, Kodak failed to make a significant impact.

Furthermore, Kodak also faced legal battles that significantly impacted its brand image. In the 1980s, the company was sued by Polaroid for patent infringement over instant photography. Kodak was forced to pay $925 million in damages to Polaroid, which damaged its reputation and financial stability. Additionally, Kodak faced a lawsuit in the 1990s over the company's decision to use the same chemicals used to produce nuclear weapons in its manufacturing processes. The lawsuit led to negative media attention and a tarnished brand image.

Kodak's inability to pivot and adapt to the changing market and technology and legal battles resulted in the company's decline. The company filed for bankruptcy in 2012 and has since restructured its business model to focus on printing and imaging technologies. Although Kodak is still a well-known brand, its association with outdated technology and legal battles has impacted its reputation and market share. Kodak's story is a reminder that it is essential to stay relevant and adapt to changes in the market to avoid the fate of being a failed business.

3. RadioShack

RadioShack was once a popular electronics retailer but failed to keep up with the changing times. The company's brand became associated with outdated technology and struggled to compete with online retailers like Amazon. RadioShack filed for bankruptcy twice, and its stores have since been closed.

RadioShack was founded in 1921 and has been a staple of the electronics industry for decades. However, the company's inability to keep up with the changing times eventually led to its downfall. In 2015, the company filed for bankruptcy after it could not compete with online retailers like Amazon and Best Buy. Despite efforts to revamp its brand and stores, RadioShack could not regain its footing and filed for bankruptcy in 2017.

One of RadioShack's biggest mistakes was failing to adapt to the shift toward mobile devices. As smartphones and tablets became more popular, the demand for traditional electronics components decreased. RadioShack's focus on selling electronic components and accessories became outdated, and the company struggled to compete with larger retailers with more diverse product offerings. This lack of innovation hurt the company's brand image and made it difficult to attract new customers.

Another factor contributing to RadioShack's demise was its lack of investment in e-commerce. As more and more consumers began shopping online, RadioShack was slow to establish a strong online presence. The company's website was outdated and did not offer the same level of convenience as competitors like Amazon. RadioShack's failure to invest in e-commerce hurt its brand image and made it less attractive to consumers looking for a convenient shopping experience. By the time the company began to invest in e-commerce, it was already too late, and its brand had been damaged.

4. Toys "R" Us

Toys "R" Us was a popular toy retailer for decades. However, the company's brand became associated with high prices and outdated stores. It struggled to compete with online retailers like Amazon and Walmart. Toys "R" Us eventually filed for bankruptcy in 2017, and its stores have since been closed.

Toys "R" Us is a classic example of how a company's branding can affect its success. The company's brand was once associated with a magical shopping experience that catered to children's fantasies. However, over time, the company failed to evolve with the changing consumer behavior and market trends.

Toys "R" Us was slow to embrace e-commerce, and its online store was clunky and difficult to navigate. This made it difficult for customers to shop online and created an uneven shopping experience. Additionally, the company's brick-and-mortar stores became outdated and were often cluttered and difficult to navigate, leading to an unpleasant shopping experience for customers.

Furthermore, Toys "R" Us failed to differentiate itself from its competitors. The company's pricing was often higher than other retailers, and it failed to offer unique products or services. It also struggled to compete with online retailers who could offer the same products at a lower price. As a result, customers had little incentive to shop at Toys "R" Us, which contributed to its eventual downfall.

5. Sears

Sears was once a dominant force in the retail industry. However, the company failed to keep up with the changing times. Sears struggled to compete with online retailers like Amazon and Walmart, and its stores became associated with outdated merchandise and poor customer service. Sears filed for bankruptcy in 2018, and many stores have since been closed.

Once a leading retail giant, Sears was established in 1893 and had a long-standing reputation for its catalog sales and brick-and-mortar stores. However, Sears slowly embraced the digital revolution as the retail industry shifted towards e-commerce. The company failed to invest in its online platforms, leading to declining sales and customer loyalty. The lack of innovation in its branding strategy caused Sears to lose relevance with its audience, resulting in its eventual bankruptcy.

Moreover, Sears' brand also suffered due to its reputation for poor customer service. The company failed to prioritize customer satisfaction, which led to a significant decline in its reputation. Long wait times, unresponsive staff, and a lack of personalized service were some of the customers' complaints about the brand. This damaged Sears' brand image and impacted the company's bottom line.

Furthermore, Sears also faced criticism for its product quality. The brand's focus on cost-cutting measures led to a decline in the quality of its merchandise. This made customers hesitant to buy from Sears, affecting their trust in the brand. Moreover, the company's inability to keep up with the latest fashion trends and consumer preferences also affected its sales. All these factors, combined with the brand's lack of innovation and poor customer service, contributed to Sears' eventual downfall.

The Importance of Keeping Personal Branding Up-to-Date

Personal branding is an essential aspect of building a successful career or business. It involves creating a unique and authentic image that represents who you are, what you stand for, and what you can offer to the world. The key to successful personal branding is consistency and relevance. You must maintain your brand image and keep it up-to-date to reflect your current achievements, skills, and goals. This section will discuss the importance of keeping personal branding up-to-date and the benefits it can bring to your professional life.

1. Stay relevant in your industry

In today's fast-paced business world, staying relevant is crucial to succeed. Your personal brand must keep up with the latest industry trends and changes. Updating your skills, knowledge, and experience is essential to remain relevant in your industry. If you do not keep your branding up-to-date, you risk becoming outdated and irrelevant. Keeping your personal brand fresh and relevant help you stay on top of your game and stand out from your competition.

2. Highlight your achievements

Personal branding is not just about creating a positive image. It is also about showcasing your achievements and successes. If you have accomplished significant milestones in your career or business, updating your branding to reflect these achievements is essential. This will help you establish yourself as a leader in your industry and build credibility with potential clients, employers, and partners.

3. Attract new opportunities

Keeping your branding up-to-date can open doors to new opportunities. You may miss out on potential job offers, partnerships, or clients if your brand is outdated. However, updating your branding can attract new opportunities that align with your current career goals and aspirations. By keeping your branding up-to-date, you can increase your visibility and establish yourself as an expert in your field.

4. Build trust and credibility

Personal branding is not just about promoting yourself but also about building trust and credibility with your audience. If your brand is outdated or inconsistent, it can undermine your credibility and make it difficult for others to trust you. Keeping your branding up-to-date can help you establish yourself as a reliable and trustworthy professional in your industry. This, in turn, can lead to more significant opportunities and stronger relationships with clients, colleagues, and partners.

5. Reinforce your values and beliefs

Personal branding is a reflection of your values, beliefs, and personality. Keeping your branding up-to-date can help reinforce your values and beliefs and ensure your brand image aligns with your personal and professional goals. By staying true to your brand, you can attract like-minded individuals who share your values and beliefs, leading to stronger and more meaningful relationships.

6. Adapt to changing circumstances

In today's rapidly changing business environment, adaptability and flexibility are essential. Keeping your branding up-to-date allows you to adapt to changing circumstances, such as a new job, a career pivot, or a shift in your industry. By updating your branding, you can pivot your brand to align with your new goals and aspirations, increasing your chances of success.

7. Stand out in a crowded market

In today's highly competitive market, standing out from the crowd is essential. Keeping your branding up-to-date helps you differentiate yourself from others and stand out in a crowded market. Creating a unique and authentic brand image can attract more attention and gain a competitive advantage over your peers.

8. Connect with your audience

Personal branding is not just about promoting yourself but also about connecting with your audience. By keeping your branding up-to-date, you can create a deeper connection with your audience and build stronger relationships with them.

This can lead to more significant opportunities, increased loyalty, and a more engaged following.

9. Keep your brand message consistent

Consistency is crucial to successful personal branding. If your brand message is inconsistent or unclear, it can confuse your audience and undermine credibility. By keeping your branding up-to-date, you can ensure that your brand message remains consistent across all channels and platforms, reinforcing your brand identity and increasing your chances of success.

10. Rebrand strategically

Personal branding is not a one-time event; it is an ongoing process. As you grow and evolve, your brand may need to be rebranded strategically to reflect your changing goals and aspirations. By rebranding strategically, you can refresh your brand image and stay relevant in your industry, attracting new opportunities and building stronger relationships with your audience.

However, rebranding should be done thoughtfully and strategically to avoid confusing or alienating your audience. Keeping your branding up-to-date can help you identify when a rebrand is necessary and execute it successfully.

CHAPTER 3

THE ELEMENTS OF PERSONAL BRANDING

Creating a strong personal brand is more important than ever in today's digital world, where first impressions are often made online. Whether you're a freelancer, entrepreneur, or simply looking to advance your career, a well-crafted personal brand can help you stand out from the crowd and achieve your goals. But what exactly is personal branding, and how can you build a powerful brand that accurately represents who you are and what you stand for?

In this chapter, we'll explore the essential elements of personal branding, from defining your unique value proposition to creating a consistent visual identity and building a strong online presence. By the end of this chapter, you'll have a solid understanding of the key ingredients that make up a successful personal brand, and you'll be equipped with the tools and knowledge you need to start building your brand with confidence and clarity.

Who You Are

As a business professional, understanding who you are is the foundation of your brand. Your personal brand is the unique combination of your personality, values, strengths, and experiences that sets you apart. It makes you unique and defines how you approach your work and interact with others.

To build a strong personal brand, starting by taking a deep look at yourself and identifying your unique qualities is important. This requires self-reflection, introspection, and a willingness to embrace your strengths and weaknesses.

One way to begin this process is by identifying your values. What are the guiding principles that shape your worldview and drive your decision-making? Is it honesty, integrity, creativity, or something else entirely? Identifying your core values can help you better understand what motivates you and how you approach your work.

Another important aspect of your brand is your personality. Are you outgoing and extroverted, or more reserved and introverted? Do you have a strong sense of humor, or are you more serious? These personality traits can help you connect with others and build meaningful relationships.

Your strengths and experiences are also key elements of your personal brand. What are you particularly good at? What unique skills or talents do you possess? What experiences have shaped you and contributed to your personal growth and development?

As you explore these different aspects of your identity, it's important to remember your professional goals and the audience you want to reach. For example, to establish yourself as an expert in a particular field, you may want to emphasize your knowledge and expertise. On the other hand, if you're looking to build a more personal brand, you may want to focus on your personality and the unique qualities that make you who you are.

Ultimately, the key to building a strong personal brand is authenticity. Your brand should be a true reflection of who you are, and it should align with your values and goals. When you're authentic to yourself, you'll naturally attract the right audience and build meaningful relationships.

In addition to being authentic, it's also important to present yourself consistently. This means developing a clear and cohesive brand message that communicates who you are and what you stand for. Whether you're networking, creating content, or interacting on social media, your message should be consistent and on-brand.

Finally, it's important to be intentional about building your brand. This means taking an active role in shaping how others perceive you and being strategic in your actions to build your brand. This may include developing a content strategy, networking with others in your field, or seeking opportunities to showcase your skills and expertise.

3 Words to Describe You

Confident

Confidence is a key trait that sets successful people apart from the rest. It is a characteristic that exudes strength and inspires trust in others. If there were three words to describe me, "confident" would be one of them. Believe in your abilities and take on challenges with a positive attitude, knowing that you can overcome any obstacle that comes your way. This assurance will help you achieve many goals and build a strong personal brand.

Being confident doesn't mean that you are arrogant or overly self-assured. On the contrary, you recognize your limitations and strive to improve yourself constantly. However, you don't let your flaws or mistakes bring you down. Instead, you learn from them and use them as opportunities for growth. This approach will give you a healthy dose of self-esteem, which is crucial to your personal and professional success.

Finally, confidence is contagious. When people see that you are confident in yourself and your abilities, they trust you more and have more faith in what you do. This has helped you build strong relationships with your colleagues, clients, and partners and will be instrumental in advancing your career. By being confident, you will be able to establish yourself as a leader in your industry and build a personal brand that is respected and admired by many.

Innovative

Innovative is one of the three words that perfectly describe who you are. You always strive to think outside the box and develop new and creative ideas that set you apart from others. You're never satisfied with the status quo and always look for ways to improve and innovate in every aspect of your life. Whether at work or in your personal life, you have a knack for finding new solutions to old problems and enjoy experimenting with new approaches.

Your innovative nature is evident in the way you approach challenges. You don't let obstacles deter you; you're always looking for ways to overcome them. You're not afraid to take risks, and you know that failure is just a stepping stone to success. You're constantly learning and growing and always willing to try new things and take on new challenges.

Your innovative mindset is also reflected in your brand. You're not content with blending in with the crowd; you want to stand out and make a lasting impression. You're always looking for new ways to showcase your unique skills and talents and are not afraid to take bold steps to achieve your goals. You know that your personal brand reflects who you are, and you want to ensure that it captures your innovative spirit and sets you apart.

Resilient

Resilient is a powerful word that describes a person who can bounce back from adversity, stay focused on their goals, and keep pushing forward even in the face of challenges. As a language model, I don't have personal experiences, but I understand the importance of resilience in developing a strong personal brand. In today's fast-paced and unpredictable world, being resilient can help you stand out from the crowd and succeed personally and professionally.

One way to cultivate resilience is to develop a growth mindset, which means approaching challenges with a positive attitude and a willingness to learn from mistakes. Embracing failure as an opportunity to learn and grow can help you build confidence, improve your skills, and become more resilient. By adopting a growth mindset, you can turn setbacks into stepping stones and use your experiences to become a stronger, more capable person.

Another way to cultivate resilience is to focus on your self-care. Taking care of yourself physically, mentally, and emotionally can help you stay grounded and resilient, even in adversity. Prioritizing exercise, nutrition, sleep, and stress management can help you build a strong foundation for your brand, allowing you to show up as your best self in all aspects of your life. Remember that resilience doesn't mean experiencing stress or challenges but having the tools and mindset to navigate them with grace and confidence.

These three words perfectly describe who you are and what you bring. You exude confidence in everything you do, whether tackling a new project or meeting new people. You approach challenges with an innovative mindset, always looking for creative solutions to problems. And when things don't go as planned, you are resilient and bounce back stronger than ever. These traits are key to your personal brand and set you apart from others in your field. As you continue to develop your brand, remember to showcase these qualities and let them shine through in everything you do.

Your Audience – Who Are They?

When it comes to personal branding, knowing your audience is crucial. After all, you're not creating a brand for yourself in a vacuum. Your brand exists to serve a specific audience, and without understanding who that audience is, you won't be able to create a personal brand that resonates with them.

So, who is your audience? The answer to that question will vary depending on what you do, but here are some general categories of people you may want to consider:

1. Your clients/customers

If you run a business, your clients or customers are likely the most important audience to consider. Who are they? What are their needs and pain points? What do they value? What are they looking for in a product or service like yours? Understanding your clients or customers is essential to creating a brand that speaks to them and meets their needs.

When understanding your clients or customers, start by identifying who they are is essential. What are their demographics? What do they do for a living? Where do they live? What are their interests and hobbies? The more you can narrow down your audience and create a detailed profile of who they are, the better you'll be able to create a personal brand that speaks directly to them.

Another important consideration for your clients or customers is their pain points. What problems are they looking to solve? What challenges are they facing in their personal or professional lives? By understanding their pain points, you can create a personal brand that positions you as someone who can solve their problems.

In addition to understanding your clients or customers' pain points, it's also important to consider what they value. What do they care about? What motivates them? What are their goals and aspirations? By tapping into these values, you can create a personal brand that aligns with their beliefs and positions you as someone who shares their values.

Finally, don't forget to consider your clients or customers' journey. From the moment they hear about your brand to the point where they become loyal customers, what steps are they taking? What questions are they asking? What obstacles are they encountering along the way? By understanding their journey, you can create a personal brand that provides value at every stage and positions you as a trusted and reliable source of information and solutions.

2. Your colleagues/industry peers

If you work in a particular industry, it's important to consider your colleagues and peers as part of your audience. What do they value? What do they think of you and your work? What are they looking for in a professional connection? Building a strong personal brand within your industry can help you establish yourself as a thought leader and create new growth opportunities.

When considering your colleagues and industry peers as part of your audience, it's important to remember the unique challenges and opportunities that come with professional networking. These individuals are not just potential clients or customers but also valuable sources of information, advice, and support. Building relationships with your colleagues and peers can help you stay up-to-date on the latest trends and developments in your industry and provide valuable insights and feedback on your work.

Professional associations and networking events are one way to connect with your colleagues and peers. These events provide opportunities to meet and connect with other professionals in your field and learn more about your industry's latest trends and best practices. Attending these events and engaging with other attendees can build relationships to help you grow your brand and achieve your professional goals.

Another important aspect of connecting with your colleagues and peers is staying active on popular social media platforms in your industry. Twitter, LinkedIn, and other social media platforms can be powerful tools for building your personal brand and connecting with other professionals in your field. By sharing valuable content, engaging in discussions, and connecting with other users, you can establish yourself as a thought leader in your industry and build a strong network of contacts.

Ultimately, the key to building a strong personal brand among your colleagues and peers is to stay engaged, active, and visible. Attend industry events, participate in online discussions, and share your knowledge and expertise with others whenever possible. By doing so, you can build a reputation as a trusted and respected member of your industry and establish yourself as a valuable resource for others in your field. Whether you're looking to grow your business, advance your career, or simply expand your network of professional contacts, connecting with your colleagues and peers is an essential part of personal branding.

3. Your social media followers

Social media is a key component of personal branding in the digital age. Your social media followers are an audience in and of themselves, and understanding who they are is critical to creating content that resonates with them. What kind of content do they engage with most? What are their interests and values? How can you use your social media presence to build a stronger connection with your followers?

Regarding personal branding in the digital age, social media followers can be a crucial audience to consider. Unlike other audiences, social media followers have chosen to follow you and engage with your content voluntarily. This makes them a highly engaged audience that can help you amplify your message and expand your reach.

To truly connect with your social media followers, it's important to take the time to understand who they are. This can involve analyzing your social media metrics to see who is engaging with your content, what kind of content they engage with the most, and what time of day they're most active. This data can help you tailor your social media strategy to better meet the needs of your followers and increase engagement.

Another important consideration when it comes to social media followers is authenticity. People are more likely to engage with authentic and genuine content, so it's important to be true to yourself and your values when creating social media content. This means being transparent about who you are, what you stand for, and what you believe in. It also means being open to feedback and criticism and engaging with your followers respectfully and authentically.

Finally, building a strong personal brand on social media requires consistency. This means posting regularly and engaging with your followers consistently. It also means maintaining a consistent brand voice and aesthetic across social media channels. By staying consistent and engaging with your followers regularly, you can build a strong social media presence that helps you connect with your audience and grow your personal brand over time.

4. Your network

Finally, don't forget about your personal network. This includes friends, family members, and acquaintances who may not be directly related to your work but still impact your brand. What do they think of you? What are their perceptions of your strengths and weaknesses? Building a strong personal brand isn't just about what you do professionally – it's about who you are, including your relationships.

Your network is vital to your brand because it allows you to showcase who you are outside of your professional life. Your network includes friends, family, and acquaintances who have seen you grow and evolve. They are a reflection of your character, values, and personality.

When building a personal brand, it's important to leverage your network. Your network can help you spread the word about your brand, connect you with new opportunities, and provide valuable feedback on your brand image. They can also help you stay grounded and authentic in your branding efforts, reminding you of who you are and where you come from.

One of the best ways to leverage your network is by creating opportunities for them to be involved in your brand. This could mean inviting them to events with you, sharing your content on social media, or simply conversing with them about your brand. By involving your network in your branding efforts, you can build a stronger sense of community around your brand and increase your reach.

Finally, remember that your network reflects your brand and vice versa. As you build your brand, it's important to stay true to who you are and your values. Your network will be watching and supporting you every step of the way, so create a brand that you can be proud of and that accurately reflects who you are.

Once you clearly understand your audience, you can start creating a personal brand that speaks directly to them. This might involve developing a unique brand voice, creating content that addresses their needs and interests, or building a network of connections within your industry. Whatever approach you take, remember that your audience should always be at the forefront of your mind. Without them, your brand won't have the power to truly make an impact.

What Do You Want to Be Known For?

As human beings, we all have a deep desire to be known and remembered for something. This is where personal branding comes in – it's about creating a unique identity for ourselves that sets us apart from others and helps us achieve our goals.

But what do you want to be known for? What is your unique selling point, and how can you use it to build your brand?

First and foremost, you need to identify your strengths and skills. What are you good at, and what sets you apart from others? This could be anything from your creative talent to your analytical skills, ability to communicate effectively, or exceptional problem-solving abilities.

Once you've identified your strengths, it's time to focus on using them to create value for others. This is where your brand comes to life. By showcasing your unique abilities and talents, you can create a lasting impression in the minds of those around you.

Regarding personal branding, it's important to be authentic to yourself. Don't try to be someone you're not – people will see right through it. Instead, focus on being the best version of yourself, and let your unique personality shine through.

Another key aspect of personal branding is consistency. You need to be consistent in how you present yourself to the world, whether through your online presence or in-person interactions. This consistency helps to build trust and credibility with your audience, which is essential for building a strong personal brand.

Ultimately, what you want to be known for is up to you. It could be a specific skill or talent or something more intangible, like your values or vision for the future. Whatever it is, ensure it's authentic, consistent, and aligned with your goals and aspirations.

Define Your Unique Value Proposition

Now that you have identified what you want to be known for, it's time to define your unique value proposition. Your unique value proposition sets you apart from others in your field and gives you a competitive edge. It's the reason why someone should choose you over someone else.

To define your unique value proposition, identify your strengths and skills. Ask yourself, what are you good at? What sets you apart from others? What unique perspective do you bring to the table? Once you have identified your strengths, consider how they can benefit your target audience. What problems can you solve for them? How can you make their lives easier or better?

Next, take a look at your competitors. What are they offering? How are they positioning themselves? Identify the gaps in the market and see where you can fill them. Consider what makes you different and how to leverage that to your advantage.

It's important to keep in mind that your unique value proposition should be concise and memorable. You should be able to communicate it in one or two sentences. Avoid using jargon or industry-specific terms that your target audience may not understand. Instead, use language that is simple and easy to understand.

Your unique value proposition should also be authentic. It should reflect who you are and what you stand for. Don't try to be someone you're not or pretend to have skills you don't. This will only lead to disappointment and dissatisfaction in the long run.

Finally, test your unique value proposition. Share it with friends, family, and colleagues and see how they react. Do they understand it? Does it resonate with them? Use their feedback to refine and improve your unique value proposition.

Remember, your unique value proposition is the foundation of your personal brand. It's what sets you apart and makes you memorable. Spend time crafting it and refining it until it's perfect.

Build Your Online Presence

Having a strong online presence is crucial to building a successful personal brand. The internet has made showcasing your skills, talents, and expertise easier to a global audience. Here are some tips to help you build a strong online presence:

1. Create a website: Your website is your digital home. It's where people will learn more about you, your brand, and what you have to offer. Ensure your website is well-designed, easy to navigate, and includes all the relevant information about you and your brand.

2. Start a blog: A blog is a great way to showcase your knowledge and expertise in your field. Write high-quality blog posts on topics your target audience finds valuable and shareable.

3. Be active on social media: Social media platforms like LinkedIn, Twitter, and Instagram are great for building your brand. Choose the platforms that make the most sense for your brand, and be consistent in your messaging and content.

4. Engage with your audience: Building a strong personal brand is about building relationships. Engage with your audience by responding to comments, sharing their content, and providing value.

5. Create valuable content: Whether it's a blog post, a video, or a podcast, create content that provides value to your target audience. Make sure your content is informative, engaging, and shareable.

6. Monitor your online reputation: Your reputation is important, and you should always be aware of what people say about you and your brand. Monitor your social media accounts and Google search results regularly, and respond to negative comments or reviews professionally and constructively.

7. Network with others in your industry: Building relationships with others in your industry can help you grow your personal brand and expand your reach. Attend industry conferences, join professional organizations, and participate in online communities to connect with others and learn from their experiences.

Building a strong personal brand is about being authentic and consistent in your messaging and actions. By following these tips and staying true to yourself and your brand, you can establish yourself as a trusted and respected authority in your field. Your online presence reflects your brand, so be intentional and strategic in your approach to building it.

Cultivate Your Network

One of the most crucial elements of personal branding is the ability to cultivate your network. Your network can be a valuable asset to your personal brand, as it can provide you with opportunities for growth and advancement.

To cultivate your network, identify the people who can help you achieve your goals. These can be people within your industry, colleagues, mentors, or even friends and family members with connections that can benefit you. Once you have identified these people, contact them and start building relationships.

Networking events and social media platforms are great places to build your network. Attend industry conferences and events, join relevant online groups, and connect with people on social media platforms like LinkedIn. Be sure to be genuine in your interactions and show a genuine interest in the people you meet.

It's also essential to maintain your network by keeping in touch with your connections regularly. Regular check-ins, sharing relevant industry news or updates, and offering to help others in your network can go a long way in building strong and lasting relationships.

Finally, remember that networking is a two-way street. Be willing to help others in your network, and they will likely be willing to return the favor. By cultivating your network and building strong relationships, you can enhance your personal brand and increase your chances of success.

Choosing Your Branding Elements (Logo, Colors, Fonts, etc.)

Your branding elements are the visual representation of your personal brand. They help you stand out in a crowded market and communicate your brand identity to your target audience. Choosing the right branding elements is critical to building a strong personal brand that resonates with your audience. Here are some key elements to consider:

Logo

Your logo is the face of your brand. It should be unique, memorable, and instantly recognizable. Your logo should reflect your brand personality and values. It should be versatile and easily adaptable across different platforms and mediums.

Colors

The colors you choose for your personal brand can have a powerful impact on how your brand is perceived. Color psychology is an important consideration when choosing your brand colors. Different colors can evoke different emotions and convey different meanings. Choose colors that align with your brand personality and values.

Fonts

Your choice of fonts can also play a role in the perception of your brand. Fonts can convey a sense of professionalism, playfulness, or elegance, among other things. Choose fonts that are easy to read and align with your brand personality.

Imagery

The imagery you use on your website, social media, and other marketing materials can also impact your personal brand. Use high-quality images that are relevant to your brand and resonate with your target audience. Be consistent in your use of imagery to create a cohesive brand identity.

Tone and Voice

Your brand tone and voice are also important branding elements. They help to communicate your brand personality and values. Decide on a tone and voice that aligns with your brand, and use it consistently across all your communications.

Tagline

A tagline is a short, memorable phrase that summarizes your brand message. It should be catchy, memorable, and communicate the essence of your brand. Your tagline should be aligned with your brand personality and values.

CHAPTER 4

SOCIAL MEDIA IN BRANDING

Social media has revolutionized how we interact with one another and completely transformed the branding landscape. In today's digital age, a strong online presence is essential for building a successful personal brand. Social media has opened up new avenues for businesses and individuals to connect with their audience on a deeper level and create a more personalized experience for their followers.

This chapter explores the power of social media in branding. It provides valuable insights into using social media to enhance your brand and achieve greater success in your career. From building a loyal following to creating engaging content, this chapter offers a comprehensive guide to harnessing the full potential of social media in your branding efforts. Whether you're an entrepreneur, influencer, or simply looking to enhance your brand, this chapter will provide the tools and strategies you need to succeed in today's digital world.

Building a Strong Personal Brand on Social Media Platforms (Steps)

Social media has become an essential tool for building a strong personal brand. With millions of users on social media platforms, it's crucial to have a solid social media presence that represents your brand and resonates with your target audience. Building a personal brand on social media platforms can help you establish credibility, attract new opportunities, and differentiate yourself. This chapter will discuss some strategies to help you build a strong personal brand on social media platforms.

1. Define Your Personal Brand

The first step in building a strong personal brand on social media platforms is to define your brand identity. You should clearly understand who you are, what you stand for, and what sets you apart from others in your industry. This will help you create a consistent brand message across all social media platforms.

Defining your brand is the foundation of building a strong online presence. Your personal brand should reflect your values, beliefs, and expertise. Start by identifying your unique strengths and skills, and consider how to leverage them to differentiate yourself from others in your industry. Your personal brand should also align with your career goals and aspirations.

To define your brand, start by creating a personal mission statement. This statement should summarize what you stand for and hope to achieve. It should be concise and memorable, and it should capture the essence of your brand. Your mission statement should guide everything you do online, from the content you share to how you interact with your followers.

Once you have your mission statement, think about your target audience. Who are you trying to reach with your brand? What are their needs and pain points? Understanding your target audience is essential to creating a personal brand that resonates with them. You should tailor your content and messaging to address their needs and interests. By defining your brand and understanding your target audience, you can create a strong online presence that sets you apart from the competition.

2. Choose the Right Social Media Platforms

With so many social media platforms available, choosing the right ones that align with your personal brand and target audience is essential. Each platform has unique strengths and weaknesses, so you should focus on the most relevant to your brand. For example, if you're a visual artist or photographer, you may want to focus on platforms like Instagram and Pinterest.

Choosing the right social media platforms to focus on is crucial for building a strong personal brand. While being present on every platform is tempting, this can be time-consuming and ineffective. It's essential to focus on the platforms that align with your brand's message and resonate with your target audience. For example, LinkedIn may be the best platform to focus on if your brand focuses on business-to-business (B2B) services, as it caters to professionals and businesses.

It's also crucial to consider the demographics of each social media platform when choosing where to focus your efforts. Different platforms attract different age groups, genders, and interests. For instance, if your target audience is mainly women aged 18-24, then you may want to focus on platforms like Instagram, TikTok, or Pinterest, as they have a higher concentration of that demographic.

Another factor to consider when choosing the right social media platform is the type of content you plan to share. Some platforms are more suited to visual content, such as images and videos, while others are better for written content, such as blog posts or articles. If your brand focuses on sharing visual content, platforms like Instagram, TikTok, and YouTube may be the best options for you. On the other hand, if your brand focuses on written content, platforms like LinkedIn, Medium, and Twitter may be more appropriate

3. Create a Consistent Brand Image

Consistency is key when building a personal brand on social media. Your profile picture, header image, bio, and content should all work together to create a consistent brand image. You should use the same color scheme, fonts, and imagery across all social media platforms to create a cohesive look and feel.

Consistency is key when it comes to building a personal brand on social media platforms. Your followers should be able to recognize your brand instantly, whether they see your profile picture, header image, or content. That's why it's important to create a consistent brand image that aligns with your brand identity. You should choose a color scheme, fonts, and imagery that reflect your brand's values, personality, and message.

Your brand image should also be visually appealing and professional. Your profile picture and header image should be high-quality and reflect your brand identity. You can use a logo, a professional headshot, or an image that represents your brand. Your content should also be visually appealing, with high-quality images and graphics that align with your brand's style and message.

Remember, your brand image should be consistent across all social media platforms. This means using the same color scheme, fonts, and imagery across all your social media profiles. Consistency helps to create a cohesive look and feel that makes it easier for your followers to recognize and remember your brand. Creating a consistent brand image can establish a strong and recognizable personal brand on social media platforms.

4. Share Valuable Content

To build a strong personal brand on social media platforms, you must provide value to your audience. This means sharing content that educates, entertains, or inspires your followers. You can share your content, curate content from other sources, or combine both. You should also ensure your content is relevant to your brand and target audience.

One of the critical aspects of building a strong personal brand on social media platforms is sharing valuable content. Your content should educate, entertain, or inspire your audience while relevant to your brand and industry. Valuable content can come in various forms, including blog posts, videos, infographics, podcasts, etc.

To create valuable content, you should first understand your target audience's pain points and interests. This will help you create content that speaks directly to and engages their needs. You should also research and analyze what type of content performs well in your industry and adapt it to fit your brand.

Furthermore, it's essential to have a content strategy that aligns with your personal brand and social media goals. This will help you plan and create consistent content that resonates with your audience. A well-defined content strategy will help you save time and resources while increasing your social media reach and engagement.

5. Engage with Your Followers

Social media is a two-way conversation, so engaging with your followers is essential. Respond to comments, thank people for sharing your content, and ask for feedback. This will help you build a community around your brand and establish trust with your audience.

Engaging with your followers is not only about responding to comments and thanking people for sharing your content. It's also about initiating conversations and asking your audience for their opinions. By asking questions, you can gain valuable insights into your audience's needs and preferences, which can help you create more relevant and engaging content. You can also use polls and surveys to get feedback and involve your audience in the content creation process. Remember to listen to your audience and be open to their feedback, as it can help you improve your personal brand and social media strategy.

Another way to engage with your followers is by recognizing their contributions to your brand. Whether featuring user-generated content or giving shoutouts to your most engaged followers, showing appreciation can help you build a strong community around your brand. You can also collaborate with your followers by inviting them to participate in contests or challenges, which can help you create buzz and increase engagement. By involving your audience in your brand's journey, you can create a sense of ownership and loyalty that can benefit your brand in the long run.

6. Network with Others in Your Industry

Social media is an excellent tool for networking and building relationships with others in your industry. Follow thought leaders and influencers in your industry, share their content, and engage with them. This will help you build a network of people who can support and promote your brand.

Networking with others in your industry is an excellent way to learn about new opportunities, stay up to date with industry trends, and expand your brand's reach. You can find like-minded professionals and peers on social media platforms such as LinkedIn, Twitter, and Facebook groups.

When networking on social media platforms, it's crucial to approach it with a mindset of giving first. Share valuable insights, answer questions, and offer support to others in your industry. By being generous with your time and knowledge, you'll build relationships with people who can help you in the future. Remember that networking is not just about what you can get out of it but also about how you can help others in your network.

7. Monitor Your Online Reputation

Your brand is not only what you share on social media platforms but also how others perceive you. You should monitor your online reputation by regularly checking what people say about you on social media. If someone leaves a negative comment, respond to it professionally and try to resolve the issue.

In addition to regularly monitoring your online reputation, it's also essential to take steps to protect it. One way to do this is by being mindful of what you share on social media platforms. Think twice before posting anything considered controversial, offensive, or inappropriate. Remember that everything you share on social media platforms reflects your brand.

Another way to protect your online reputation is by acting against any false or defamatory statements about you on social media platforms. If someone spreads false information about you, you can ask them to remove it. You can also report the content to the social media platform's administrators, who may remove it if it violates their community guidelines. Taking swift and professional action against any negative online comments or reviews can help protect your personal brand's reputation and ensure that your online presence remains positive and professional.

Building a strong personal brand on social media takes time and effort, but it's worth it in the long run. By following these strategies, you can establish a credible and trustworthy personal brand that resonates with your target audience. Remember to stay authentic, provide value, and engage with your followers to build a strong community around your brand.

Leveraging Social Media for Effective Brand Storytelling

Social media has become indispensable for businesses to establish a strong brand identity and connect with their target audience. With the growing popularity of platforms like Facebook, Instagram, Twitter, and LinkedIn, businesses can now leverage social media for effective brand storytelling. Brand storytelling is about communicating your brand's values, vision, and mission to your audience compellingly and engagingly. It helps build an emotional connection with your audience, crucial for building brand loyalty and driving sales.

One of the key benefits of using social media for brand storytelling is that it allows businesses to reach a large audience quickly and easily. Social media platforms have millions of active users, meaning businesses can connect with their target audience at a previously unimaginable scale. Moreover, social media allows businesses to target specific demographics and interests, ensuring their brand messaging reaches the right people at the right time.

Businesses need to develop a solid social media strategy to leverage social media effectively for brand storytelling. A social media strategy outlines the goals and objectives of your social media presence and the tactics you'll use to achieve them. It's important to align your social media strategy with your overall brand strategy, ensuring your social media messaging is consistent with your brand identity.

Visual content is one of the most effective ways to tell your brand story on social media. Visual content is highly engaging and can quickly capture your audience's attention. Platforms like Instagram and Pinterest are particularly suited to visual storytelling, with businesses using these platforms to showcase their products and services visually appealingly. However, even on platforms like Twitter and LinkedIn, businesses can use visual content like images and videos to supplement their brand messaging.

Another key aspect of effective brand storytelling on social media is authenticity. Social media users are savvy and can quickly spot inauthentic messaging. Therefore, businesses need to ensure that their brand messaging is genuine and authentic, reflecting their values and mission. Social media is an excellent platform for showing the human side of your brand, highlighting the people and stories behind your products and services.

Businesses need to engage with their audience on social media actively. Social media is a two-way conversation, and businesses need to be responsive to their audience's needs and feedback. By actively engaging with their audience, businesses can build stronger relationships with their customers, driving loyalty and advocacy.

Maximizing Social Media Channels to Amplify Brand Awareness

Social media has become an integral part of our daily lives. From catching up with friends and family to exploring the latest trends, it's pervasive in our personal and professional worlds. Social media has also emerged as a powerful tool for businesses looking to amplify their brand awareness. In this chapter, we'll explore the different social media channels and the strategies that can help you maximize your presence on each platform to build a strong personal brand.

Social Media Channels

Social media is not a one-size-fits-all platform. Each channel has its unique audience, features, and algorithms. Understanding these differences is crucial to effectively reach your target audience and maximizing your brand's visibility. Here's an overview of the most popular social media channels and how you can leverage them to promote your brand:

1. Facebook

Facebook is the world's largest social network, with over 2 billion active users. It is a great platform for connecting with friends and family, but it can also be a powerful tool for personal branding. Facebook allows you to create a page for your personal brand and share content with your audience. Here are some tips to maximize your presence on Facebook:

- Consistently post engaging content that resonates with your audience
- Use Facebook Live to connect with your followers in real-time
- Join Facebook groups related to your niche to network with other professionals and increase your visibility

2. Instagram

Instagram is a visual platform that allows you to share photos and short videos with your followers. With over 1 billion active users, it's an excellent platform for personal branding, especially if your brand is visually oriented. Here are some tips to maximize your presence on Instagram:

- Use high-quality visuals that align with your brand's aesthetic
- Utilize Instagram Stories to share behind-the-scenes glimpses of your life and work
- Use relevant hashtags to increase your visibility and reach a wider audience

3. LinkedIn

LinkedIn is a professional networking platform with over 700 million users. It's the perfect platform for personal branding, especially if you're in a B2B industry. Here are some tips to maximize your presence on LinkedIn:

- Create a strong LinkedIn profile that highlights your skills and expertise
- Publish articles and posts to position yourself as a thought leader in your industry
- Use LinkedIn groups to network with other professionals in your niche

4. Twitter

Twitter is a real-time platform that allows you to share short messages with your followers. With over 300 million active users, it's an excellent platform for building brand awareness and engaging with your audience. Here are some tips to maximize your presence on Twitter:

- Tweet regularly and engage with your followers
- Use relevant hashtags to join conversations and increase your visibility
- Share industry news and insights to position yourself as a thought leader

5. YouTube

YouTube is a video-sharing platform that allows you to create and share videos with your audience. With over 2 billion monthly active users, it's an excellent platform for personal branding, especially if you're comfortable in front of the camera. Here are some tips to maximize your presence on YouTube:

- Consistently create high-quality videos that align with your brand's message
- Use YouTube Live to connect with your audience in real-time
- Collaborate with other YouTubers in your niche to increase your visibility

Crafting a Good Social Media Strategy

Once you've identified the social media channels that align with your brand, it's time to craft a social media strategy. Here are some key steps to help you create an effective social media strategy:

1. Define Your Goals

What do you want to achieve with your social media presence? Do you want to build brand awareness, drive traffic to your website, or generate leads? Defining your goals will help create a focused and effective social media strategy.

2. Identify Your Target Audience

Who is your target audience? What are their needs, interests, and pain points? Understanding your audience will help you create content that resonates with them and build a strong online community.

3. Create Engaging Content

Your social media strategy should create engaging and relevant content that resonates with your audience. This can include blog posts, videos, images, infographics, and more. Make sure your content aligns with your brand's message and values.

4. Consistency is Key

Consistency is key when it comes to social media. Regularly posting high-quality content will help you build a loyal following and increase your visibility. Use a content calendar to plan your posts and ensure you post regularly.

5. Engage With Your Audience

Engagement is crucial to building a strong personal brand on social media. Respond to comments, messages, and mentions to build a relationship with your audience. This will help you build trust and loyalty with your followers.

6. Track Your Results

Tracking your social media metrics is important to understand what's working and what's not. Use analytics tools to track your engagement, reach, and other metrics. Use this data to refine your strategy and improve your results over time.

Engaging Your Target Audience through Social Media Branding Strategies

Social media is an excellent tool for branding and building a personal brand. However, it is essential to note that social media platforms are not just channels to promote and sell products or services. They are also platforms to engage with customers and build long-term relationships. This section will discuss how to engage your target audience through social media branding strategies.

1. Consistency in Branding

Consistency in branding is crucial to creating a strong online presence. Your brand should have a consistent look and feel across all social media platforms. This consistency includes your brand colors, logo, tone, and messaging. Ensure your brand message aligns with your brand values and reflects your target audience's needs.

2. Create Quality Content

Quality content is essential in engaging your target audience. Create content that resonates with your target audience and aligns with your brand's messaging. The content should be relevant, informative, and valuable to your audience. Use visual content, including images and videos, to make your content more engaging.

3. Utilize Influencer Marketing

Influencer marketing is an effective way to reach a broader audience and engage with your target audience. Identify influencers in your industry or niche and collaborate with them to promote your brand. Influencers have a loyal following, and their endorsement of your brand can boost your credibility and increase your brand's reach.

4. Build a Community

Building a community on social media is an excellent way to engage with your target audience. Encourage your followers to share their thoughts and opinions on your brand and create a space where they can interact with one another. Respond to their comments and messages to create a sense of community and show that you value their feedback.

5. Use Hashtags

Hashtags are an excellent way to reach a broader audience and engage with your target audience. Use relevant hashtags that align with your brand and content. Hashtags make it easy for your audience to find your content and participate in discussions related to your brand.

6. Offer Value to Your Audience

Offering value to your audience is an excellent way to engage with them and build long-term relationships. Provide them valuable information, tips, and advice about your brand or industry. Offer exclusive discounts or promotions to your social media followers to show that you value their loyalty.

7. Monitor and Respond to Feedback

Monitor your social media channels regularly and respond to feedback promptly. Address negative feedback and complaints in a professional and timely manner. Responding to feedback shows that you value your audience's opinions and are willing to address their concerns.

Measuring the Success of Your Social Media Branding Campaigns

Social media platforms are essential to branding campaigns in today's digital world. They allow businesses to connect with their target audience and promote their brand cost-effectively and efficiently. However, measuring the success of social media branding campaigns can be challenging. In this section, we will discuss some of the key metrics that can help you determine the success of your social media branding campaigns.

1. Engagement Metrics

Engagement metrics are a great way to measure the success of your social media branding campaigns. These metrics measure how your audience interacts with your content, such as likes, comments, shares, and followers. By analyzing engagement metrics, you can determine which type of content resonates with your audience and adjust your future campaigns accordingly.

For instance, if your Instagram post receives many likes and comments, your audience finds your content appealing. On the other hand, if your post receives low engagement, it may indicate that you need to reevaluate your content strategy.

2. Reach Metrics

Reach metrics measure the number of people who have seen your content. The higher your reach, the more people you can convert into customers. These metrics can be used to determine the effectiveness of your social media branding campaigns in increasing brand awareness.

For instance, if your Facebook page reaches many people, your branding campaign effectively reaches your target audience. If your reach is low, it may indicate that you need to adjust your targeting or content strategy.

3. Conversion Rate

Conversion rate is another crucial metric for measuring the success of your social media branding campaigns. It refers to the percentage of people who take a desired action after seeing your content, such as purchasing or filling out a form. To measure conversion rates, you can use tools like Google Analytics, which tracks website traffic and user behavior.

To improve your conversion rate, ensuring that your social media content is aligned with your overall brand messaging and provides value to your audience is essential. You should also ensure your website is user-friendly and optimized for conversions, with clear calls-to-action and easy navigation.

3. Brand Awareness

Brand awareness measures how familiar your target audience is with your brand. It is an essential metric to track because it can influence consumer behavior and purchase decisions. To measure brand awareness, you can use surveys and social listening tools that track mentions of your brand across social media platforms.

You should create consistent and cohesive branding across all your social media channels to improve brand awareness. You can also leverage social media advertising to increase visibility and reach a broader audience.

4. Return on Investment (ROI)

ROI measures the return you receive on your investment in a social media branding campaign. It is calculated by comparing the revenue generated by the campaign to the cost of running it. To calculate ROI, you need to track your campaign's metrics, such as reach, engagement, and conversion rates, and then compare them to your business's revenue.

To improve ROI, you should create social media content aligning with your business goals and strategy. You should also continually monitor and optimize your campaigns to ensure you get the most value from your investment.

Why Every Brand Should Take Social Media Serious

Whether it's to stay in touch with friends and family or stay up to date on the latest news, social media has revolutionized how we interact with the world around us. But social media isn't just a tool for personal use. It has become an indispensable tool for businesses to reach and engage with customers. Here's why every brand should take social media seriously.

Increased Visibility

Social media provides a platform for brands to increase their visibility and reach a wider audience. With over 4 billion active social media users worldwide, social media offers a vast potential audience for businesses. Businesses can increase their brand awareness and attract new customers by using social media platforms like Facebook, Instagram, Twitter, and LinkedIn. Social media also allows businesses to target specific demographics and reach a more niche audience, which can be incredibly valuable for businesses looking to reach a specific market.

Social media can also drive traffic to a business's website, essential for generating leads and increasing conversions. By sharing links to their website on social media, businesses can encourage their followers to visit their sites and learn more about their products or services. This increased traffic can also positively impact a business's search engine rankings, as search engines like Google consider website traffic when ranking sites in search results.

Social media can also help businesses build brand awareness by creating a consistent brand presence across all social media channels. By regularly posting high-quality content that aligns with their brand's values and messaging, businesses can build a strong brand identity that resonates with their audience. This increased brand awareness can also translate into increased brand loyalty and customer retention, as customers are likelier to stick with a brand they feel connected to.

Businesses that take social media seriously can gain a competitive advantage over those that don't. Social media has become an essential part of the customer experience, and businesses that don't have a strong social media presence risk falling behind their competitors. By investing in social media marketing, businesses can stay relevant and top-of-mind with their audience and differentiate themselves from their competitors. This competitive advantage can be particularly important for small businesses, which may not have the marketing budget of larger corporations.

Increased Engagement

Social media is not only a platform for businesses to promote their products or services but also for engagement. Social media allows businesses to interact with their customers in real-time, respond to comments and messages, and build relationships with their audience. Businesses can build trust, loyalty, and a sense of community around their brand by engaging with their customers on social media.

One of the most significant advantages of social media is the increased engagement it provides for businesses. Social media platforms offer a unique opportunity for businesses to connect with their customers more personally and engagingly. For example, businesses can create engaging content like videos, infographics, and blog posts to share with followers. These posts can help businesses educate their customers about their products or services and provide value to their audience.

Another way social media increases engagement is by providing businesses with real-time communication with their customers. Social media allows businesses to respond instantly to comments and messages, creating a two-way conversation. This open communication channel helps businesses build trust and loyalty with their customers, as they can quickly address any concerns or questions.

Social media also allows businesses to personalize customer engagement, making them feel valued and appreciated. By creating a more personalized experience, businesses can make their customers feel more connected to their brand, increasing brand loyalty and advocacy. For example, businesses can use social media to celebrate milestones, birthdays, or other special occasions with their customers, creating a sense of community around their brand.

Cost-Effective Marketing

Social media is also a cost-effective marketing tool for businesses. Traditional marketing methods like print, radio, and television ads can be expensive and ineffective. On the other hand, social media marketing can be done for a fraction of the cost, making it an excellent option for businesses on a budget. Social media marketing can also be more targeted, allowing businesses to reach their desired audience more effectively.

One of the most significant advantages of social media for businesses is that it is a cost-effective marketing tool. Many social media platforms, such as Facebook, Twitter, Instagram, and LinkedIn, allow businesses to create free accounts and pages to promote their products or services. This means businesses can reach millions of potential customers without spending a penny on advertising or marketing costs.

In addition to free social media accounts, social media platforms offer paid advertising options to target specific audiences based on demographics, interests, behaviors, and more. These paid advertising options can be significantly less expensive than traditional advertising methods, such as print, radio, and television ads. For example, businesses can run a Facebook ad campaign for as little as a few dollars daily and reach a highly targeted audience.

Furthermore, social media advertising provides businesses with a high return on investment (ROI). With social media advertising, businesses can track the effectiveness of their campaigns in real time, seeing how many people clicked on their ads, how many converted into customers, and how much revenue their ads generated. This allows businesses to adjust their advertising strategies to optimize their ROI, ensuring they get the most bang for their buck. In summary, social media marketing offers a cost-effective way for businesses to reach their target audience, build their brand, and grow their business.

Brand Reputation Management

Social media is an essential tool for businesses to manage their brand reputation. With social media, businesses can quickly respond to negative feedback or complaints, addressing any issues and demonstrating their commitment to customer service. Social media also allows businesses to monitor what people say about their brand online, allowing them to address any potential issues before they become bigger problems.

Brand reputation management is crucial for businesses of all sizes. Social media platforms provide a unique opportunity for businesses to monitor their reputation in real time and respond to negative comments or feedback. By addressing these issues quickly and professionally, businesses can demonstrate their commitment to customer satisfaction, build trust with their audience, and prevent minor issues from turning into major problems.

One key aspect of brand reputation management on social media is proactive monitoring. This involves regularly monitoring social media channels for mentions of your brand, products, or services. Using tools like social media listening software, businesses can track brand mentions, sentiment, and engagement, allowing them to respond quickly to comments or feedback. This can help businesses stay on top of potential issues and address concerns before they escalate.

Another important aspect of brand reputation management on social media is transparency. Social media users expect businesses to be transparent and honest about their products and services. This means being upfront about any issues, providing timely updates, and promptly responding to customer complaints or feedback. By being transparent on social media, businesses can build trust with their audience and establish a positive brand reputation, even in the face of negative feedback or criticism.

Opportunity for Innovation

Social media is constantly evolving, so there's always an opportunity for innovation. Businesses that embrace social media can experiment with new marketing techniques, engage with their audience in new ways, and explore new growth opportunities. By staying current on the latest social media trends and best practices, businesses can stay ahead of the curve and continue to grow their brand.

Social media platforms provide businesses with a unique opportunity for innovation. By experimenting with new marketing techniques and engagement strategies, businesses can keep their audience engaged and stay ahead of the competition. Social media platforms constantly evolve, with new features and trends emerging regularly. Businesses that stay updated and embrace these changes can differentiate themselves from their competitors and attract new customers.

One area where social media provides an opportunity for innovation is content creation. Social media users are constantly bombarded with content, so businesses need to find ways to stand out. By creating engaging and shareable content, businesses can capture their audience's attention and increase their reach. Social media platforms offer various tools and features for creating innovative content, such as Instagram's Reels or TikTok's video editing features.

Another area where social media provides an opportunity for innovation is customer engagement. Social media platforms offer businesses a unique opportunity to engage with their audience in real time. By responding to comments, messages, and feedback promptly and professionally, businesses can build trust with their audience and establish a sense of community around their brand. Social media platforms also offer a range of interactive features, such as polls, quizzes, and live streaming, which businesses can use to engage with their audience in new and exciting ways. By embracing these features, businesses can stand out from competitors and keep their audience engaged.

CHAPTER 5
MAKING YOUR BRAND CATCHY AND ATTRACTIVE

Creating a personal brand can be a powerful tool for advancing your career and achieving your goals. However, simply having a brand is not enough in today's competitive landscape. Your brand must be catchy and attractive to stand out from the crowd and capture the attention of your target audience.

This chapter will explore the secrets to creating a brand that is memorable and resonates with your audience. We'll cover everything from developing your unique value proposition to crafting a compelling brand story that showcases your skills and expertise. Whether you're just starting to build your personal brand or looking to take it to the next level, the insights and strategies in this chapter will help you create a brand that truly captures the power of personal branding.

What Makes a Brand Catchy?

To succeed in personal branding, you need a brand that is not only memorable but also catchy and attractive. But what exactly makes a brand catchy? Here are some key factors to consider:

1. Unique Value Proposition

Your unique value proposition is the foundation of your brand. It is your promise to your audience that no one else can deliver. To develop a compelling UVP, identify your target audience and their pain points, needs, and desires. Then, consider how your skills, experience, and personality can help solve their problems or fulfill their desires in a unique and valuable way. Your UVP should be clear, concise, and focused on the benefits you provide to your audience. It should also be tailored to your niche or industry and highlight what makes you stand out. By developing a strong UVP and integrating it into all aspects of your personal brand, you can create a powerful and memorable brand that resonates with your target audience.

2. Consistency

Consistency is key to building a catchy brand. Everything should be consistent and cohesive, from your brand message to your visual identity. Your audience should be able to recognize your brand at a glance, no matter where they encounter it. Consistency builds trust and helps establish your brand as a reliable and credible authority in your field.

Inconsistencies can confuse your audience and dilute your brand's messaging. Therefore, you must ensure that all aspects of your brand remain consistent, from your logo to your content and social media presence. Consistency in your visual identity can help your audience identify your brand quickly and easily, building a sense of familiarity and trust. Consistency in your messaging can also help your audience understand what your brand stands for and what it has to offer.

A consistent brand shows that you take your business seriously and are committed to delivering a quality experience to your audience. It also ensures that your audience knows what to expect from your brand, leading to a more engaged and loyal following. Therefore, it's important to establish brand guidelines that outline the use of your logo, fonts, color palette, and messaging and to ensure that everyone involved in creating content for your brand adheres to these guidelines. Maintaining consistency across all your brand touchpoints allows you to build a cohesive and memorable brand that stands out from the competition.

3. Emotion

A catchy brand evokes emotion in its audience. Emotion is a powerful driver of behavior, and if you can make your audience feel something, they are more likely to remember and engage with your brand. Aim to create an emotional connection with your audience through your brand, whether it's excitement, inspiration, or a sense of belonging.

Regarding personal branding, emotion is a crucial element that can make or break your brand's success. Emotion is what drives people to take action, and it is what creates a lasting impression in their minds. You must understand their needs, desires, and pain points to create an emotional connection with your audience.

This requires getting to know your audience and creating content that speaks directly to them. By understanding your audience's emotions, you can craft a brand message that resonates with them and addresses their concerns. Additionally, you can use storytelling, visual elements, and other creative techniques to evoke specific emotions in your audience. For example, bright colors and playful imagery can evoke happiness and joy, while darker and somber imagery can evoke sadness or contemplation.

Overall, by tapping into the power of emotion, you can create a personal brand that not only stands out but also creates a lasting impact in the minds and hearts of your audience.

4. Simplicity

A catchy brand is simple and easy to understand. Your brand message, visual identity, and UVP should be communicated in a way that is easy to digest and remember. Avoid clutter and complexity, and aim for a clean, streamlined look and feel that is easy on the eyes and mind.

A simple brand is not only easier to remember and recognize, but it also helps to avoid confusion and clutter. A too-complex or convoluted brand can quickly overwhelm your audience and dilute your message. Therefore, aim for a clean, straightforward look and feel that conveys your brand message clearly and effectively. This can include a simple and easy-to-read logo, a limited color palette, and a consistent visual language that reflects your brand values and personality.

Simplicity also extends to your brand message, which should be communicated in a way that is concise and easy to understand. Your audience should be able to grasp your UVP and brand message within seconds of encountering your brand. Remember, simplicity does not mean sacrificing creativity or originality. Instead, it means finding the perfect balance between simplicity and creativity to create a memorable and effective brand.

5. Storytelling

A brand with a good story is inherently more memorable and engaging. A catchy brand tells a story that resonates with its audience and creates a connection with them. Your brand story should highlight your unique journey and the challenges you have overcome to get where you are today. It should also convey your values and mission in a relatable and compelling way.

Storytelling is a powerful tool that can help make your personal brand more memorable and engaging. Your brand story should be authentic and compelling, highlighting your unique journey and the challenges you have overcome to get where you are today. It should convey your values and mission in a relatable and inspiring way to your target audience. A well-crafted brand story can create an emotional connection with your audience, fostering a sense of trust and loyalty.

When developing your brand story, consider what sets you apart from others in your field, what motivates and drives you, and how you can use your experiences to make a positive impact in the lives of others. A strong brand story can serve as the foundation of your personal brand and help you stand out in a crowded market. Remember that your story is your superpower and can be a game-changer for personal branding.

6. Authenticity

Authenticity is a critical component of a catchy brand. Your audience can sense when you are insincere or inauthentic, which can quickly turn them off your brand. To build a catchy brand, be true to yourself and your values. Let your personality shine through in your brand, and don't be afraid to show your flaws and vulnerabilities.

Authenticity is crucial to a catchy brand because it establishes trust and credibility with your audience. Your audience wants to connect with people with real experiences and genuine values. Being authentic means being true to yourself and your audience and not trying to be someone you're not. It also means being transparent about your brand and your intentions.

Honesty and transparency can help you establish a loyal following of people who relate to you and believe in what you stand for. Authenticity can also help you differentiate yourself from your competitors, who may focus more on creating a polished image than being genuine. Ultimately, building a catchy brand grounded in authenticity requires you to know yourself, your values, and your audience and to communicate your brand message in a genuine, honest, and relatable way.

7. Visual Appeal

Visual appeal is a critical aspect of a catchy brand. Your visual identity should be visually appealing and memorable, including your logo, color scheme, typography, and imagery. It should also be consistent with your brand message and values. When designing your visual identity, consider your target audience and what visual elements will likely resonate with them.

Visual appeal is a critical aspect of building a catchy and attractive brand. When it comes to personal branding, your visual identity is often the first thing your audience sees and remembers about your brand. A visually appealing brand communicates professionalism, credibility, and attention to detail.

To create a visually appealing brand, paying attention to every aspect of your visual identity is important, from your logo to your color palette to your typography. Your logo should be simple, memorable, and reflective of your brand's values and mission. Your color palette should be carefully chosen to convey the mood and emotion you want your brand to evoke. Your typography should be legible and consistent with your brand's personality and style.

Additionally, high-quality and relevant imagery can help bring your brand to life and make it more engaging to your audience. A visually appealing brand makes a memorable impression and creates a sense of professionalism and trustworthiness, which can go a long way in attracting and retaining your target audience.

Brand Examples (e.g., Short, Catchy, Descriptive)

When building a personal brand, one of the most important things you can do is choose a memorable, catchy, and descriptive name. A great brand name can help you stand out from the crowd, capture the attention of your target audience, and communicate what makes you unique. In this section, we'll explore some examples of successful personal brands and what makes them so effective.

1. Marie Forleo - MarieTV

Marie Forleo is a successful entrepreneur, author, and speaker who has built a thriving personal brand around her name. One of the most effective aspects of her brand is using the name "MarieTV" for her online show. The name is catchy and descriptive, instantly communicating to her audience what the show is about - Marie sharing her insights and advice on various topics related to personal and professional development. By branding her show this way, Marie has created a memorable and easily recognizable platform that has helped her build a loyal following.

2. Gary Vaynerchuk - VaynerMedia

Gary Vaynerchuk is a well-known entrepreneur, author, and internet personality who has built a powerful personal brand over the years. One of the key elements of his brand is the name of his company - VaynerMedia. The name is short, catchy, and easy to remember, and it communicates what the company does concisely and effectively. Using his name as the basis for his brand, Gary has created a personal connection with his audience while building a successful business around his expertise.

3. Jenna Kutcher - The Goal Digger Podcast

Jenna Kutcher is a successful business coach and online personality who built a brand around her name. One of the most successful elements of her brand is her podcast - The Goal Digger Podcast. The name is catchy and descriptive, conveying that the podcast is about helping listeners achieve their goals and reach their full potential. By branding her podcast this way, Jenna has created a platform that resonates with her audience and has helped her build a loyal following of fans and customers.

4. Simon Sinek - Start With Why

Simon Sinek is a well-known author, speaker, and consultant who has built a personal brand around his name and his philosophy of "Start With Why." The name of his brand is both catchy and descriptive, immediately communicating what he stands for and what he wants to help his audience achieve. By branding his work in this way, Simon has created a powerful platform that has helped him reach a wide audience and become a thought leader in his field.

5. Rachel Hollis - Rise

Rachel Hollis is a popular author, speaker, and lifestyle personality who has built a personal brand around her name and her philosophy of "Rise." The name of her brand is short, catchy, and memorable, and it conveys the message that Rachel is all about helping her audience rise to their full potential and achieve their dreams. By branding herself this way, Rachel has built a platform that resonates with her audience and has helped her become a bestselling author and influencer.

6. Pat Flynn - Smart Passive Income

Pat Flynn is a well-known entrepreneur and online personality who has built a successful personal brand around his name and philosophy of "Smart Passive Income." The name of his brand is both catchy and descriptive, immediately conveying what he's all about - helping his audience create passive income streams through smart and strategic business practices. By branding himself in this way, Pat has been able to build a loyal following of fans and customers, and he's become a respected authority in the world of online business and entrepreneurship.

7. Gretchen Rubin - The Happiness Project

Gretchen Rubin is a bestselling author and speaker who has built a personal brand around her name and her mission to help people live happier, more fulfilling lives. The name of her brand is "The Happiness Project," which is both catchy and descriptive. The name immediately communicates what she's all about, and it's easy for her audience to remember and connect with. By branding herself this way, Gretchen has built a platform that resonates with her audience and has helped her become a trusted voice in the self-help and personal development space.

8. Tim Ferriss - The 4-Hour Workweek

Tim Ferriss is a well-known author, entrepreneur, and podcast host who built a successful personal brand around his name and philosophy of achieving maximum productivity with minimal effort. The name of his bestselling book and the basis for his brand is "The 4-Hour Workweek," which is both catchy and descriptive. The name immediately communicates what he's all about - helping people achieve more with less time and effort. By branding himself in this way, Tim has been able to build a loyal following of fans and customers, and he's become a respected authority in the world of entrepreneurship, productivity, and lifestyle design.

9. Sophia Amoruso - Girlboss

Sophia Amoruso is an entrepreneur, author, and founder of Nasty Gal, a successful online fashion retailer. She has built a personal brand around the name "Girlboss," which is both catchy and empowering. The name communicates Sophia's mission to inspire and empower women to create success and become leaders in their fields. By branding herself in this way, Sophia has built a community of like-minded women who are inspired by her message and see her as a role model and mentor.

10. Marie Forleo - Everything is Figureoutable

Marie Forleo is a motivational speaker, author, and founder of B-School, an online business training program. She has built a personal brand around the phrase "Everything is Figureoutable," which is catchy and inspiring. The phrase communicates Marie's belief that anything is possible if you're willing to work and figure out how to make it happen. By branding herself in this way, Marie has been able to attract a large and loyal following of fans and customers who are inspired by her message and see her as a trusted guide and mentor on their own personal and professional growth journeys.

What are the Purpose, Value, and Differentiation?

Creating a personal brand that is both catchy and attractive is not an easy feat. It requires a deep understanding of your purpose, value, and differentiation. In this section, we'll dive into these elements and explore how they can help you create a personal brand that stands out from the crowd.

What is the Purpose?

Before you start building your brand, it's important to understand your purpose. Your purpose is the reason why you do what you do. It's what drives you and gives meaning to your work. Understanding your purpose is crucial because it allows you to align your personal brand with your values and goals. Your purpose will also guide your decisions and actions, ensuring that everything you do aligns with your vision.

To identify your purpose, ask yourself some key questions. What motivates you? What do you want to achieve in your career and life? What are your core values? Once you clearly understand your purpose, you can start building your personal brand around it.

What is the Value?

Your personal brand should be based on the value you bring to the table. This value can be in the form of your skills, expertise, or unique perspective. Understanding your value is critical because it allows you to communicate your strengths and differentiate yourself from others in your field.

To identify your value, start by analyzing your skills and expertise. What are you good at? What sets you apart from others in your field? What unique insights do you bring to the table? Once you clearly understand your value, you can start building your personal brand around it.

What is the Differentiation?

Differentiation is what sets you apart from others in your field. It's what makes you unique and memorable.

Differentiation is important because it helps you stand out in a crowded market and captures the attention of your target audience.

To differentiate yourself, start by analyzing your competition. What are they doing well? What are they not doing well? What gaps can you fill in the market? Once you clearly understand your competition, you can start building your brand around your unique strengths and offerings.

The Power of Purpose, Value, and Differentiation

When you combine your purpose, value, and differentiation, you create a personal brand that is both powerful and attractive. Your purpose gives meaning to your work, your value communicates your strengths, and your differentiation sets you apart from others in your field. Together, these elements create a personal brand that is compelling and memorable.

By focusing on your purpose, value, and differentiation, you can create a personal brand that captures your target audience's attention and helps you achieve your goals. Your personal brand becomes a powerful tool for advancing your career and building your reputation in your field.

Don't forget; creating a catchy and attractive personal brand requires a deep understanding of your purpose, value, and differentiation. By focusing on these key elements, you can build a personal brand that stands out from the crowd and captures the attention of your target audience. Your personal brand becomes a powerful tool for achieving your goals and building your reputation in your field.

CHAPTER 6
GIVING YOUR BRAND SOME PERSONALITY

Your personal brand is more than just a logo or tagline; it's people's perception of you. To make your brand memorable and engaging, it needs to have personality. Giving your brand a personality helps you connect with your target audience on a deeper level, making it more relatable and memorable.

In this chapter, we'll explore the secrets to giving your brand personality and show you how to create a personal brand that truly reflects who you are. Whether you're looking to build a brand from scratch or refresh your existing brand, the insights, and strategies in this chapter will help you create a brand that stands out from the crowd.

Personal Branding Personality

A personal brand with personality is a brand that stands out. It's a brand that people remember, connects with, and want to engage with. However, giving your personal brand personality can be challenging. You want to make sure your brand reflects your values, but you also want to ensure it resonates with your target audience. In this section, we'll explore how to create a personal brand with a personality that truly reflects who you are and resonates with your audience.

Identify Your Unique Personality Traits

The first step to giving your brand personality is to identify your unique personality traits. This means understanding what makes you different from everyone else in your field. Your personality traits are the characteristics that define you as a person and are the foundation of your brand.

Start by asking yourself some key questions. What are your strengths and weaknesses? What are your values? What are your interests and passions? What do you want to be known for? By answering these questions, you can identify your unique personality traits and build your brand around them.

Conducting a personal branding audit is an effective way to identify your unique personality traits. This involves taking a closer look at your brand and identifying the aspects of your brand that resonate with your audience. You can also evaluate your competitors and identify what makes your brand different from theirs. Doing so can highlight your unique qualities and make them a core part of your personal brand.

Another effective way to identify your unique personality traits is to get feedback from others. Ask friends, family, colleagues, or even your target audience what they think of when they think of you. What are your best qualities? What sets you apart from others? This feedback can help you identify your strengths and weaknesses and highlight the aspects of your personality that resonate with others.

Embrace your quirks when identifying your unique personality traits. Your quirks are the things that make you stand out and make you memorable. Maybe you have an unusual hobby or a unique talent. Maybe you have a quirky sense of humor or a distinctive style. Embracing these quirks can help you differentiate yourself from others and make your brand more memorable. Don't be afraid to let your personality shine through in your brand.

Infuse Your Brand with Your Personality

Once you have identified your unique personality traits, it's time to infuse your brand with your personality. This means bringing your personality traits to life in your brand. For example, if you're creative, you might want to incorporate bold colors and imaginative designs into your brand. If you're compassionate, you might want to focus on providing excellent customer service and building strong relationships with your clients.

Your personal brand should be an extension of your personality, so it's important to be authentic to yourself. People can tell when you're not being genuine, which can hurt your brand's credibility.

Storytelling is an excellent way to infuse your brand with your personality. Sharing stories about your experiences, struggles, and successes can help people connect with you more deeply. It also helps to create an emotional connection between you and your audience. Sharing your personal stories also helps to build trust and credibility because people can relate to your struggles and see how you overcame them.

Incorporating personalized visuals is another way to infuse your brand with your personality. This can include your brand colors, fonts, and imagery representing your unique personality traits. For example, if you're a nature lover, you might want to incorporate natural imagery into your branding, such as trees, mountains, or landscapes. Personalized visuals help to create a memorable and recognizable brand that stands out in a crowded market.

Your voice is an essential aspect of your brand. It's how you communicate with your audience and share your message. Infusing your brand with your voice means using language that reflects your personality traits. For example, if you're lighthearted, you might want to use more casual language in your messaging. If you're serious, you might want to use more formal language. Incorporating your voice into your brand helps to create a consistent and authentic brand identity that resonates with your target audience.

Connect with Your Target Audience

While infusing your brand with your personality is important, it's equally important to connect with your target audience. Your personal brand needs to resonate with your audience if you want to build a loyal following. This means understanding their needs, interests, and values.

Start by identifying your target audience. Who are they? What are their pain points? What are their interests and passions? Once you clearly understand your target audience, you can start to tailor your brand to their needs.

For example, if you're targeting millennials, you might want to focus on social media and use trendy language in your messaging. If you're targeting professionals, you might want to focus on providing valuable insights and expertise in your field.

People are wired to respond to stories. Using storytelling in your personal brand can be a powerful tool for connecting with your target audience. Storytelling is a way to create an emotional connection with your audience, allowing them to see themselves in your story. It also helps you stand out and be more memorable. Share your personal journey and experiences or the stories of your clients and customers. Make sure that the stories align with your brand messaging and values.

In today's world, authenticity and transparency are highly valued. People want to connect with real people, not just a brand image. Being authentic means being true to who you are, and being transparent means being open and honest about your brand, products or services, and business practices. This builds trust and credibility with your target audience and can lead to more loyal and engaged customers.

Engaging with your target audience is important to building a personal brand with personality. This means actively participating in conversations on social media, responding to comments and messages, and being accessible to your audience. Engaging with your audience shows that you care about their opinions and feedback. It also helps you build relationships and establish yourself as an authority in your field. Take the time to listen to your audience and respond to their needs and concerns. This will help you build a strong and engaged following for your brand.

How to Develop a Personal Branding Persona

Creating a personal brand that resonates with your target audience requires more than a catchy tagline or a sleek logo. To truly connect with your audience, your brand needs personality. A personal branding persona represents your unique personality, values, and style that you project to the world. In this section, we'll explore how to develop a personal branding persona that aligns with your values and helps you connect with your target audience.

Before developing your branding persona, you need to understand your values. Your values are the beliefs and principles that guide your decision-making and shape your character. They are critical to your brand because they define who you are and what you stand for.

To identify your values, ask yourself some key questions. What motivates you? What are your core beliefs? What are the principles that guide your decision-making? Once you clearly understand your values, you can start building your personal branding persona around them.

Your branding persona should reflect your unique style. Your style is how you express yourself through appearance, behavior, and communication. Your style is important because it helps you differentiate yourself from others in your field and makes your personal brand more memorable.

Identify your unique style by analyzing your appearance, behavior, and communication. What do you wear? How do you behave in social situations? How do you communicate with others? Once you clearly understand your style, you can start building your personal branding persona around it.

Identifying your unique style, and creating a brand voice, crafting a compelling story is essential for developing a personal branding persona. Your story should illustrate your journey, struggles, achievements, and aspirations. It should highlight your unique experiences and give your audience an idea of who you are.

Your story should be authentic and relatable, something your target audience can connect with. It should also be concise and clear, allowing your audience to easily understand and remember it. A compelling story can help you build a strong emotional connection with your target audience, making them more likely to trust and follow you.

Consistency is needed to develop a personal branding persona. Your branding persona should be consistent across all your communication channels, from your website to your social media profiles to your business cards. This consistency helps establish your personal brand's identity and makes it more memorable.

Your personal branding persona should also be consistent with your behavior and actions. If your branding persona portrays you as a caring and compassionate person, then your actions should reflect that. Inconsistencies between your branding persona and your behavior can damage your brand's credibility and cause your target audience to lose trust in you.

Continuously evolve your branding persona. Your values, style, and communication style may change over time, and your brand needs to reflect these changes. Continuously evaluating your brand and making necessary adjustments can help you stay relevant and engage with your target audience.

Your branding persona should also have a unique brand voice. Your brand voice is the tone and language you use to communicate with your target audience. Your brand voice is important because it helps you establish a consistent and authentic voice across all your communication channels.

To create a brand voice, start by analyzing your communication style. How do you communicate with others? What tone do you use? What language do you use? Once you clearly understand your communication style, you can start building your personal branding persona around it.

One of the most important things to remember when developing your branding persona is to stay authentic. Your personal branding persona should truly represent who you are and what you stand for. It should not be a persona you put on to try and impress others.

To stay authentic, ensure your personal branding persona aligns with your values, style, and communication style. Don't try to be someone you're not; your brand will come across as disingenuous.

Remember that evolving your personal branding persona doesn't mean you must completely overhaul it. You can make small adjustments and tweaks to ensure your personal brand remains consistent and relevant. Regularly evaluating and updating your personal brand will help ensure that it continues to reflect accurately who you are and what you stand for.

Creating Consistency Across All Branding Channels

Your brand should be recognizable across all channels, whether your website, social media platforms, business cards, or any other marketing materials you use. Consistency in branding helps to build trust with your audience, which is essential for developing long-lasting relationships with your clients and customers.

To create consistency in your personal branding, define your brand's visual and verbal identity. Your visual identity includes your logo, color scheme, typography, and imagery. Your verbal identity includes your brand's tone of voice, messaging, and values.

Once you have defined your brand's visual and verbal identity, it's time to ensure consistency across all your branding channels. Here are some tips to help you achieve this:

1. Use the Same Logo

Use the same logo across all channels and formats, including online and offline materials. However, ensuring that the logo is consistent in different file formats is also crucial. Whether it is a JPG, PNG, or PDF file, the logo should have the same design, size, and color. This consistency will ensure that your logo looks professional and uniform, regardless of where it is used.

Your logo should be scalable and adaptable to different sizes and dimensions. Your logo should look great when it's small, such as on a business card or social media profile, and also when it's large, such as on a billboard or brochure. By designing a scalable logo, you can maintain consistency across all channels and avoid losing the visual impact of your brand.

Another important aspect to consider when using the same logo is ensuring it is compatible with different backgrounds. For example, if your logo has a white background and you place it on a black or dark blue background, it may not be visible or legible. Ensure that your logo has a transparent background, allowing it to blend in seamlessly with any color scheme or design element. This will maintain consistency and professionalism across all channels, whether on your website, social media platforms, or marketing materials.

2. Stick to the Same Color Scheme

Your brand's color scheme should also be consistent across all channels. Choose a primary and two or three secondary colors and use them consistently throughout your branding materials.

Creating a brand style guide is one way to ensure consistency in your color scheme. This document outlines your brand's visual identity, including your logo, color scheme, typography, and imagery. It serves as a reference for you and anyone who works with your brand to ensure they consistently use the correct colors. You can include information such as color codes, Pantone colors, and RGB values to make it easy for everyone to use the same colors across all channels.

When choosing your brand's colors, consider how they make your audience feel. Different colors evoke different emotions, and you want to ensure your color scheme aligns with your brand's personality and values. For example, blue is often associated with trust and reliability, while yellow is associated with happiness and optimism. Consider the message you want to convey and choose colors that align with that message.

Another way to maintain consistency in your color scheme is to limit the number of colors you use. Too many colors can be overwhelming and confusing for your audience. Stick to a primary and two or three secondary colors, and use them consistently across all channels. You can also use shades and tints of your chosen colors to add depth and variety to your branding materials while maintaining consistency. Limiting your color palette can create a cohesive and recognizable brand presence.

3. Use the Same Typography

Your brand's typography should be consistent across all channels. Choose two or three fonts and use them consistently on your website, social media platforms, business cards, and any other marketing materials.

When selecting typography for your personal brand, consider the font's readability and legibility. It's important to use fonts that are easy to read, especially when it comes to important information, such as headlines or calls to action. Sans-serif fonts are often a good choice for digital platforms, as they are easy to read on screens and have a modern, clean look. On the other hand, serif fonts are often used in print materials as they are more traditional and convey a sense of sophistication.

Another important aspect of using the same typography is maintaining font size and weight consistency. This means using the same font size and weight for your branding channels for headers, subheadings, body text, and captions. This consistency helps to create a sense of hierarchy and organization in your branding materials, making them easier to read and navigate for your audience.

To add visual interest and variety to your typography while maintaining consistency, consider using different font styles within your chosen family. For example, you can use a bold weight for headlines and a regular weight for body text. This creates a sense of contrast and hierarchy while maintaining consistency in your typography. Additionally, using a different font for emphasis or quotes can add interest and variety to your branding materials as long as it aligns with your overall brand identity.

4. Use the Same Imagery

Your brand's imagery should also be consistent across all channels. Use the same style of photography or illustrations on your website, social media platforms, business cards, and any other marketing materials.

When selecting imagery for your personal brand, choosing images that align with your brand's visual identity and messaging is important. Your imagery should reflect the personality and values of your brand and should be consistent across all channels. For example, if you're a wellness coach, you may want to use images that show people doing yoga or meditating to create a calming and peaceful atmosphere.

Another way to ensure consistency in your imagery is to use the same style of photography or illustrations. If you're using photography, consider the images' lighting, color scheme, and composition. If you're using illustrations, consider the style and level of detail. Using the same imagery style across all channels, you can create a cohesive and recognizable brand presence.

If you're struggling to find the right imagery for your brand, consider creating your own. With the rise of social media platforms like Instagram and TikTok, creating your images and videos has never been easier. You can use your smartphone to take high-quality photos and videos and edit them using free or low-cost apps. By creating your imagery, you can ensure that it aligns with your brand's visual identity and messaging and is unique to your brand.

5. Develop a Tone of Voice

Your brand's tone of voice should be consistent across all channels. Develop a brand voice that reflects your personality and values, and use it consistently in all your messaging.

Your brand's tone of voice is how you communicate with your audience through your messaging. Choosing a tone of voice that reflects your brand's personality and values is important. Are you formal or casual? Professional or playful? Think about how you want your audience to perceive your brand and choose a voice that aligns with that perception. Your tone of voice should be consistent across all channels to create a cohesive brand presence.

One way to develop your brand's tone of voice is to create a brand messaging framework. This document outlines your brand's core messaging, including your brand's mission, values, and unique selling proposition. It also includes guidelines for your brand's tone of voice, such as the type of language and phrasing you use. A brand messaging framework serves as a reference for you and anyone who works with your brand to ensure that your messaging is consistent across all channels.

When creating your brand's tone of voice, consider the language you use. Your language should be simple and easy to understand, regardless of your industry or audience. Avoid jargon or technical language that your audience may not understand. Instead, focus on communicating your message clearly and concisely. Use words and phrases that resonate with your audience and align with your brand's values. By using clear and concise language, you can develop a tone of voice that is consistent and easy for your audience to understand.

6. Use the Same Messaging

Your brand messaging should also be consistent across all channels. Develop a core message that communicates what your brand stands for, and use it consistently in all your marketing materials.

Using the same messaging across all your branding channels is crucial for creating a strong and consistent brand presence. Your brand messaging should be clear, concise, and memorable. It should communicate your brand's unique value proposition and differentiate you from competitors.

To ensure consistency in your messaging, develop a core message that communicates what your brand stands for. This message should be easy to understand and remember. Once you have your core message, use it consistently in all your marketing materials, including your website, social media platforms, business cards, and any other materials you use to promote your brand.

Another way to ensure consistency in your messaging is to focus on the benefits your brand offers. Rather than just listing features, highlight how your brand solves problems for your customers or clients. By focusing on benefits, you create a more emotional connection with your audience and make it easier for them to see the value of your brand. This approach also helps you stand out from your competitors, who may focus only on features.

7. Be Consistent in Posting

Posting consistently helps create a consistent brand presence. Develop a posting schedule that works for you and sticks to it. Post consistently on your website, social media platforms, and other channels to promote your brand.

Posting always is an excellent way to provide value to your audience. By sharing relevant and valuable content, you position yourself as an expert in your field and establish trust with your audience. Consistent posting also lets you showcase your brand's personality and values, which can help you attract new followers and customers.

Posting consistently is not only important for creating a consistent brand presence, but it's also essential for staying engaged with your audience. By consistently posting on your website, social media platforms, and other channels, you show your audience that you are committed to your brand and care about their needs. Your audience will come to expect regular updates from you, and if you fail to deliver, you risk losing their attention and interest.

Posting can always be challenging, especially if you have a busy schedule. However, you can make things easier by automating your posting schedule. Many tools allow you to schedule your posts in advance, such as Hootsuite, Buffer, and Sprout Social. By automating your posting schedule, you can ensure your brand is consistently represented across all channels, even if you cannot post manually daily. This also helps you save time and stay organized, allowing you to focus on other important aspects of your brand.

Real People, Real Connections

As a business professional, you already know how important it is to give your brand a personality. You want your brand to stand out, be memorable, and connect with your audience. But how can you do that? The answer lies in real people and real connections.

When we talk about real people, we mean your customers, clients, and followers. They are the ones who will ultimately decide if your brand is successful or not. That's why listening to them, understanding their needs, and building relationships with them are crucial.

One way to build a connection with your audience is to be authentic. You need to be true to yourself and your brand. Don't try to be something you're not. If your brand is fun and quirky, let that shine through in your messaging. If your brand is more serious and professional, don't try to make jokes that don't fit your brand's tone. Authenticity builds trust, and trust builds loyal customers.

Another way to connect with your audience is to create content that resonates with them. That means understanding what they care about and what they're looking for from your brand. Don't just create content for the sake of creating content. Make sure it provides value to your audience. Whether it's educational, entertaining, or inspirational, make sure it's something they want to see.

But building connections with your audience isn't just about what you do online. It's also about what you do offline. If you can meet your customers or clients in person, take advantage of it. Attend conferences, host events, or even just grab coffee with some of your followers. Meeting people in person can solidify your relationship and make it even stronger.

But it's not just about building connections with your audience. It's also about building connections with other people in your industry. Networking is crucial for any business professional, but it's even more important when building a personal brand. You never know who might be able to help you or who might become a valuable mentor or friend.

Your brand is not just about you. It's about the people who support you and believe in you. Show appreciation for your followers and customers. Respond to their comments and messages. Share their content and give them shoutouts. They will care more about you when you show that you care about them.

Additionally, when building real connections, it's important to remember that it's a two-way street. Don't just focus on what your audience can do for you; focus on what you can do for them. Be a resource for them by sharing valuable information and offering solutions to their problems. Engage with them on social media by responding to comments and messages and reposting their content. Showing that you care about your audience and their needs will create a more mean-ingful connection that can lead to long-term loyalty.

Another way to build real connections is by creating a community around your brand. This can be done through social media groups, online forums, or in-person events. Bringing together people with a common interest or passion can create a sense of belonging and foster deeper connections. Encourage your community members to share their thoughts and experiences, and provide opportunities for them to connect. When your brand becomes a hub for like-minded individuals, it can become even more powerful.

Finally, don't be afraid to show your personality and quirks. People want to connect with other people, not with faceless corporations. Share your personal stories and experiences, and let your unique voice shine through in your content. By showing your human side, you can create a deeper connection with your audience beyond just a transactional relationship. And remember, it's okay to make mistakes and show vulnerability. Your audience will appreciate your honesty and authenticity, and it can even make your brand more relatable.

The Motivation Behind Your Personal Brand

Your brand is more than just a logo or a catchy tagline. It represents who you are, what you stand for, and what motivates you. Understanding the motivation behind your brand is key to creating a powerful and authentic image. In this section, we'll explore some common motivations behind personal brands and how to use them to give your brand some personality.

Career-focused Branding

One of the most common motivations behind personal branding is career advancement. Whether you're an entrepreneur, a freelancer, or a corporate employee, you want to be recognized as an expert in your field. You want to build a reputation as knowledgeable, skilled, and trustworthy. By creating a personal brand that showcases your expertise, you can position yourself as a thought leader and attract new opportunities.

If career advancement is your main motivation, create content demonstrating your skills and knowledge. Share your insights and experiences through blog posts, social media updates, and industry publications. Attend networking events and conferences to connect with others in your field. And don't be afraid to showcase your achievements, such as awards, certifications, or successful projects.

If career advancement is your main motivation behind personal branding, showcasing your unique strengths and value proposition is essential. You need to stand out from the crowd and demonstrate why you're the best person for the job. One way to do this is by creating a strong online presence that showcases your skills and accomplishments. Build a website or LinkedIn profile highlighting your education, certifications, and relevant work experience.

In addition to creating content demonstrating your expertise, networking with others in your industry is crucial. Attend conferences, join professional associations, and engage with others in your field on social media. Make an effort to build relationships with influencers and thought leaders, as they can help you gain exposure and credibility. And don't forget to ask for referrals and recommendations from clients or colleagues who are happy with your work.

Finally, to build a personal brand that focuses on your career advancement, continuously learning and growing is important. Stay up-to-date on the latest trends and innovations in your industry. Invest in professional development and attend workshops or seminars that can help you enhance your skills. By demonstrating your commitment to learning and improvement, you can position yourself as a top candidate for any job or opportunity that comes your way.

Charity and Cause-based Branding

Another motivation behind personal branding is to make a difference in the world. Whether through a specific cause, such as environmental conservation or social justice or through supporting a particular charity or non-profit organization, your personal brand can be a powerful tool for creating change.

If you're motivated by a specific cause or charity, create content that raises awareness and inspires action. Share statistics, stories, and personal experiences that illustrate the importance of your cause. Partner with organizations that align with your values and donate some of your profits or time to support their efforts. Using your personal brand to promote a cause you care about can make a real impact in the world.

When it comes to charity and cause-based branding, authenticity is crucial. If you're using your personal brand to support a particular cause, it's important to genuinely care about that cause and to take action to make a difference. Consumers can quickly spot insincere efforts, and it can damage your brand's reputation. Ensure that your brand aligns with the cause you're supporting and that you're doing more than just using it for marketing purposes.

Partnering with other like-minded individuals and organizations can effectively amplify your charity or cause-based brand. Seek out non-profits, charities, and other organizations that share your values and work together to achieve your common goals. Collaborating with these groups can expand your reach, generate more awareness, and increase donations to your chosen cause. You can also organize events, webinars, or workshops together to educate and engage with your audience.

You can leverage social media platforms to create a community around your charity or cause-based brand. Use hashtags and tag other relevant accounts to increase the visibility of your content. Create posts encouraging your followers to take action, such as signing a petition, donating to a charity, or volunteering their time. Share user-generated content from your followers who are also passionate about the cause, as it can help you build a sense of community and authenticity around your brand.

Influencer Branding

Another motivation behind personal branding is the desire to become an influencer. Whether in a specific industry, such as beauty or fitness, or a broader sense, as a lifestyle influencer, building a personal brand can help you gain a following and influence others.

To become an influencer, focus on creating content that resonates with your audience. Share your personal experiences, recommendations, and insights that align with your niche or industry. Collaborate with other influencers or brands to expand your reach and credibility. And engage with your followers by responding to comments and messages and building a community around your brand.

Influencer branding can be a powerful way to build a personal brand that reaches a large audience. One key strategy for building influence is to create engaging, informative, and entertaining content. This can take many forms, from social media posts to blog articles, podcasts, or videos. The key is to find the format that resonates with your audience and delivers value to them.

Another important aspect of influencer branding is building relationships with influencers in your niche or industry. This can help you expand your reach, gain credibility, and access new opportunities. Consider contacting other influencers or brands that align with your values and goals. Collaborate on projects, share each other's content, or attend events together to build a community around your personal brand.

Finally, staying true to your values and message as an influencer is important. Building influence can be tempting, but it's essential to ensure that you're promoting products or ideas that align with your personal brand and values. Be transparent about any sponsored or affiliate content with your audience, and only promote products or services you truly believe in. This will help you build a loyal and engaged audience and create a personal brand that truly reflects your identity.

Examples of Strong Brands (Company/Personal)

Building a strong brand is essential for success in any business. From global corporations to personal brands, a strong brand can significantly impact an audience. Let's look at some examples of strong brands and what makes them stand out.

Company Brands

Apple

One of the most iconic brands in the world, Apple has built its reputation on innovation, design, and user experience. From its sleek product designs to its attention to detail in packaging and marketing, Apple has created a brand synonymous with quality and luxury. The company's commitment to simplicity and user-friendly interfaces has created a loyal fan base that anticipates every new product launch.

Nike

Another iconic brand, Nike, is known for its "Just Do It" slogan and its focus on empowering athletes. Nike has successfully built a brand that represents both performance and style. The company's partnerships with high-profile athletes and celebrities have helped to establish its reputation as a leader in the athletic apparel industry. Nike has also taken a stand on social issues, such as its support for Colin Kaepernick, which has resonated with younger consumers who value brands that align with their values.

Coca-Cola

Coca-Cola is one of the most recognizable brands in the world. The company has built its brand around its refreshing and delicious beverages, but it is also known for its marketing campaigns that evoke feelings of happiness and joy. Coca-Cola's brand is characterized by its iconic logo, signature red and white color scheme, and memorable jingles and slogans.

Tesla

Tesla has disrupted the automotive industry by building electric cars that are stylish, high-performance, and environmentally friendly. The company's brand is built around innovation, sustainability, and luxury. Tesla's logo, which features a stylized "T," is instantly recognizable, and the company's commitment to creating a cleaner, more sustainable future has earned it a loyal fan base.

Amazon

Amazon has revolutionized the retail industry by offering a massive selection of products, fast and reliable shipping, and excellent customer service. The company's brand is built around convenience, selection, and affordability. Amazon's logo, which features an arrow that points from "A" to "Z," suggests that the company offers everything from A to Z. Amazon has also expanded into other industries, such as streaming video and cloud computing, which has helped to diversify its brand.

Red Bull

Red Bull has built its brand around energy, adrenaline, and extreme sports. The company's energy drinks are marketed to boost performance and provide a "wing" to help people achieve their goals. Red Bull's brand is characterized by its edgy and adventurous marketing campaigns, which feature extreme sports athletes performing stunts and taking risks.

Disney

Disney is a brand that is synonymous with entertainment, storytelling, and magic. The company has built its brand around its iconic characters, movies, and theme parks. Disney's brand is characterized by its fun and whimsical aesthetic, commitment to quality, and ability to evoke nostalgia and childhood memories. Disney's logo, which features the iconic Mickey Mouse ears, is instantly recognizable.

Starbucks

Starbucks has built its brand around coffee culture, creating a social experience around drinking coffee. The company's stores are designed to be inviting and comfortable, and its baristas are trained to provide excellent customer service. Starbucks' brand is characterized by its premium quality coffee, sustainability commitment, and innovative products, such as the Pumpkin Spice Latte.

These company brands have successfully built a strong brand identity by focusing on key values and qualities that resonate with their audience. They have developed a clear visual identity, messaging, and tone of voice consistent across all their channels. By understanding what makes these brands stand out, you can apply these principles to your brand and create a compelling brand identity that connects with your audience.

Personal Brands

Gary Vaynerchuk

A well-known entrepreneur and social media personality, Gary Vaynerchuk has built his brand around his marketing and business expertise. His straight-talking style and focus on providing value to his audience have earned him a loyal following. Vaynerchuk has also built a media empire with a popular podcast, books, and a digital media company, VaynerMedia. His success has made him a sought-after speaker and consultant.

Marie Forleo

Another successful entrepreneur and media personality, Marie Forleo, has built her personal brand around her message of "everything is figureoutable." Her focus on mindset and personal development has resonated with her audience, and she has built a community around her brand through her popular YouTube channel, podcast, and courses. Forleo has also written a best-selling book and is a sought-after speaker.

Seth Godin

Seth Godin is a marketing guru and bestselling author who has built his brand around his marketing and entrepreneurship expertise. His blog, books, and speeches have earned him a reputation as one of the most respected and influential voices in the marketing world. Godin's focus on building authentic connections with his audience has helped him build a loyal following that eagerly awaits his insights on marketing and business.

Brené Brown

Brené Brown is a researcher and author who has built her brand around her vulnerability, shame, and empathy expertise. Her TED Talk on vulnerability has been viewed millions of times, and she has written several best-selling books. Brown's focus on authenticity and vulnerability has resonated with her audience and helped her build a community of fans passionate about her message.

Tim Ferriss

Tim Ferriss is an author and entrepreneur who has built his brand around his productivity and lifestyle design expertise. His best-selling book, "The 4-Hour Work Week," has become a bible for entrepreneurs and has helped him build a loyal following. Ferriss's focus on testing and optimizing every aspect of his life has inspired his audience to do the same and helped him build a community of fans passionate about living life on their own terms.

Oprah Winfrey

Oprah Winfrey is a media mogul who has built her personal brand around her expertise in personal development, spirituality, and social issues. Her talk show, magazine, and book club have made her one of the most influential voices in the media. Winfrey's focus on authenticity and empathy has earned her a loyal following, and her commitment to giving back has helped her build a community of fans who share her values.

Tony Robbins

Tony Robbins is a motivational speaker and author who has built his brand around his personal development and self-improvement expertise. His seminars, books, and speeches have inspired millions to achieve their goals and improve their lives. Robbins's focus on taking massive action and pushing past limiting beliefs has resonated with his audience. It has helped him build a community of fans passionate about personal growth.

Gretchen Rubin

Gretchen Rubin is an author and blogger who has built her personal brand around her expertise in happiness and habit formation. Her best-selling book, "The Happiness Project," has inspired millions to take control of their lives and find happiness. Rubin's focus on the small, everyday habits contributing to happiness has resonated with her audience. It has helped her build a community of fans passionate about living a fulfilling life.

Lewis Howes

Lewis Howes is an author, podcaster, and entrepreneur who has built his brand around his business, leadership, and personal development expertise. His podcast, "The School of Greatness," has become one of the most popular podcasts in the world, and his books and courses have helped thousands of people achieve their goals. Howes's focus on vulnerability, authenticity, and personal growth has resonated with his audience and helped him build a community of fans passionate about living their best life.

Marie Kondo

Marie Kondo is a consultant and author who has built her brand around her decluttering and organization expertise. Her best-selling book, "The Life-Changing Magic of Tidying Up," has inspired millions to simplify their lives and focus on what truly matters. Kondo's focus on sparking joy and letting go of things that no longer serve us has resonated with her audience and helped her build a community of fans passionate about living a clutter-free life.

CHAPTER 7

MARKETING AND MAINTAINING YOUR EVOLVING PERSONAL BRAND

Your personal brand is a dynamic entity that evolves. Your brand identity may shift and change as you gain new skills, experience, and insights. To stay relevant and competitive in your industry, it's important to market and maintains your evolving personal brand.

In this chapter, we'll explore strategies for marketing and maintaining your brand as it evolves. From building a strong online presence to networking and collaborating with others, we'll cover everything you need to know to stay ahead of the game.

Creating a Marketing Plan for Your Personal Brand

Marketing your brand is essential for building your reputation and attracting new opportunities. But how do you create a marketing plan for your brand? This section will walk you through the steps to create a comprehensive marketing plan for your personal brand.

Define Your Objectives

The first step in creating a marketing plan for your brand is to define your objectives. What do you hope to achieve through your marketing efforts? Are you looking to attract new clients or job offers? Do you want to establish yourself as an industry thought leader? You can create a more targeted and effective marketing plan by clearly defining your objectives.

Know Your Target Audience

To effectively market your personal brand, you need to know your target audience. Who are the people that you want to reach with your marketing efforts? What are their needs and interests? By understanding your target audience, you can create content and messaging that resonates with them and attracts their attention.

Develop Your Unique Selling Proposition

Your unique selling proposition sets you apart from others in your industry. What makes you unique and valuable to your target audience? Your USP should clearly and concisely communicate what you offer and why people should choose you over others.

Choose Your Marketing Channels

You can use many different channels for marketing your personal brand, including social media, blogging, podcasting, speaking engagements, and more. It's important to choose the most effective channels for reaching your target audience and aligning with your objectives and USP.

Create a Content Strategy

Content is the cornerstone of any successful personal branding marketing plan. Your content should align with your objectives, USP, and target audience. It should also provide value to your audience and showcase your expertise and personality. Whether you create blog posts, videos, podcasts, or other types of content, it's important to have a consistent strategy for creating and sharing content that resonates with your target audience.

Set a Budget and Schedule

Once you have your marketing plan in place, setting a budget and schedule for your marketing activities is important. How much money and time can you realistically devote to marketing your personal brand? Setting a budget and schedule ensures you have the resources you need to execute your marketing plan effectively.

Measure Your Results and Adjust Your Plan

Measure the results of your marketing efforts and adjust your plan as needed. What metrics will you use to track your progress? How will you know if your marketing efforts are successful? Regularly reviewing your results and adjusting your marketing plan ensures that your personal brand continues to evolve and grow over time.

Leveraging Influencer Marketing to Build Your Brand

Social media influencers have become a significant part of the marketing landscape. They have a large following on social media platforms and have a significant impact on their followers' purchasing decisions. As a personal brand, partnering with influencers can help you reach a wider audience and build your brand. Here's how you can leverage influencer marketing to build your brand.

The first step in leveraging influencer marketing for your personal brand is identifying the right influencers. You need to find influencers whose niche aligns with your brand and whose followers are your target audience. Look for influencers whose values align with yours and whose content resonates with your brand.

Once you have identified potential influencers, research to determine their authenticity and engagement rate. You want to partner with influencers who have a genuine connection with their followers and whose followers actively engage with their content.

Once you have identified the right influencers, the next step is to build a relationship with them. Start by following them on social media platforms and engaging with their content. Comment on their posts, share their content, and tag them in your posts.

After you have built a relationship with the influencers, reach out to them with a proposal for a partnership. Ensure your proposal is compelling and highlights the benefits of working with you. You must approach influencers professionally and respectfully and be clear about your expectations.

When collaborating with influencers, it's essential to establish clear expectations and goals for the partnership. You need to agree on the type of content, the frequency of posts, and the duration of the partnership. It's also essential to agree on compensation for the influencer's work, whether monetary or in-kind.

You should also provide influencers with detailed information about your brand, target audience, and marketing goals. This will help them create content that resonates with your brand and their followers.

Measuring the success of your influencer partnerships to determine their effectiveness in building your brand is essential. You can use various metrics, such as engagement rate, reach, and sales, to determine the success of your influencer partnerships.

You should also track the performance of individual influencers to determine which ones are most effective in building your brand. This will help you identify influencers you can partner with for future campaigns.

Public Speaking and Networking to Build Your Personal Brand

Public speaking and networking are essential skills to build your brand. They allow you to connect with others and establish yourself as an expert. This section will explore the benefits of public speaking and networking and provide tips on leveraging them to build your personal brand.

The Power of Public Speaking

Public speaking is a powerful tool for building your brand. When you speak at events, you can share your expertise with a large audience and establish yourself as a thought leader in your industry. Additionally, speaking at events can help you establish valuable connections and build your network. Here are some tips on how to use public speaking to build your brand:

1. Choose the Right Events: Look for events where your target audience will be in attendance. This will help ensure that you're speaking to the right people and that your message will resonate with them.

2. Create a Compelling Presentation: Make sure your presentation is engaging and informative. Use visual aids to help illustrate your points and keep your audience engaged.

3. Practice, Practice, Practice: Practice your presentation until you're comfortable delivering it. This will help you feel more confident on stage and ensure that your message is delivered effectively.

4. Follow-Up with Attendees: After your presentation, follow up with attendees. This will help you establish connections and relationships with potential clients or partners.

Networking to Build Your Brand

Networking is another important tool for building your personal brand. It allows you to establish connections with others in your industry and create opportunities for collaboration and growth. Here are some tips on how to use networking to build your brand:

1. Attend Industry Events: Attend events and conferences related to your industry. This will allow you to meet others in your field and learn about the latest trends and developments.

2. Join Professional Organizations: Joining professional organizations related to your industry can also help you build your network. These organizations often have regular meetings and events where you can connect with others in your field.

3. Be Strategic: When networking, be strategic in who you connect with. Look for individuals who can help you advance your career or provide valuable insights into your industry.

4. Follow-Up: After networking events, follow up with individuals you've connected with. This can help you establish relationships and create opportunities for collaboration and growth.

Building Your Personal Brand Through Speaking and Networking

Both public speaking and networking are valuable tools for building your personal brand. By speaking at events and attending industry gatherings, you can establish yourself as an expert in your field and build valuable connections. Use these tips to help you leverage these tools to build your brand and advance your career.

Using PR to Build Your Personal Brand

Building and maintaining a strong personal brand is essential for success. While social media and influencer marketing are effective tools for building your brand, public relations (PR) can also be crucial in establishing your reputation and credibility. In this section, we will discuss how PR can help you build your personal brand and provide some tips for using PR to your advantage.

What is PR?

Public relations management and building relationships between an organization or individual and its target audience. PR aims to create a positive public image and enhance its reputation through earned media coverage, event sponsorships, and other public-facing activities. PR can help establish your brand by creating a consistent message across all channels and communicating your unique value proposition to your audience.

Using PR to Build Your Personal Brand

Here are some ways to use PR to build your personal brand:

1. Develop a PR strategy: Before you begin any PR efforts, developing a clear strategy is important. Identify your target audience, establish key messages, and determine what you want to achieve with your PR efforts. This will help you create a focused and effective PR plan.
2. Build relationships with the media: Building relationships with journalists and media outlets is key to getting your name and brand out there. Reach out to

reporters and influencers in your industry, offer expert commentary or write guest blog posts, and attend networking events to meet journalists face-to-face.

3. Creating compelling content that resonates with your target audience is essential to building your brand. Develop thought leadership pieces, press releases, and social media posts that showcase your expertise and unique perspective. Use storytelling to engage your audience and make your brand more relatable.

4. Leverage social media: Social media is a powerful tool for building your brand and increasing reach. Share your content across all platforms, engage with your followers, and use hashtags to increase visibility. You can also use social media to connect with journalists and influencers in your industry.

5. Get involved in your community: Involvement in your local community can help you establish yourself as a thought leader and build relationships with key stakeholders. Attend local events, sponsor community initiatives, and participate in volunteer work to get your name out there and build a positive reputation.

Measuring the Success of Your Personal Brand

Measuring the success of your brand is crucial to understanding how well your efforts are paying off. It allows you to see what's working and what's not, so you can make informed decisions about the direction you want to take your brand. In this section, we'll explore some key metrics and tools you can use to measure your personal brand's success.

Identifying Key Metrics

Before you start measuring the success of your brand, you need to determine the metrics that are most important to you. Here are some key metrics you should consider:

1. Reach: Reach measures the number of people who see your content, including your website, social media profiles, and other online platforms.
2. Engagement: Engagement measures how actively your audience interacts with your content. This can include likes, comments, shares, and other forms of engagement.
3. Influence: Influence measures how much your personal brand impacts your audience's opinions and behaviors.
4. Conversions: Conversions measure how many people take a desired action after interacting with your brand, such as signing up for your newsletter or purchasing a product.

Using Tools to Measure Your Personal Brand's Success

You can use several tools to measure your personal brand's success. Here are some popular options:

1. Google Analytics: Google Analytics is a free web analytics tool that provides insights into website traffic, user behavior, and other key metrics.
2. Social Media Analytics: Most social media platforms offer tools that track engagement, reach, and other key metrics.

3. Brand Monitoring Tools: Brand monitoring tools, such as Brand24 and Mention, allow you to monitor your brand's reputation, and track mentions across the web.

4. Surveys: Surveys can be a valuable tool for measuring your personal brand's success. You can use surveys to gather feedback from your audience and learn what they like and dislike about your brand.

Analyzing Your Results

1. Once you've identified your key metrics and started using tools to measure your personal brand's success, it's important to analyze your results. Here are some tips for analyzing your data effectively:

2. Look for Trends: Look for patterns in your data over time. Are your metrics increasing or decreasing? What factors may be contributing to these trends?

3. Compare Your Results: Compare your results to industry benchmarks and competitors' metrics. How do you stack up?

4. Set goals for improving your metrics and tracking your progress over time.

5. Adjust Your Strategy: Use your data to inform your strategy moving forward. What changes can you make to improve your metrics?

Continuing to Develop Your Skills and Expertise

Your personal brand is not only about how you present yourself but also about the value you offer. Therefore, it is essential to continue developing your skills and expertise to stay relevant and competitive. Here are some ways to do so:

Professional development opportunities include attending conferences, taking courses or workshops, or participating in industry-related events. These activities can help you stay up-to-date on industry trends, learn new skills, and network with like-minded professionals. By investing in your professional development, you can position yourself as an expert in your field, further enhancing your brand.

Networking is a great way to expand your knowledge and expertise. You can meet new people who may offer insights and knowledge in your field by attending networking events. Additionally, you may meet potential mentors or people who can provide valuable feedback on your brand. Consider joining professional organizations, attending conferences, or participating in industry-related groups online to network and stay connected.

Volunteering can be a great way to develop new skills and expertise. Consider volunteering in areas related to your personal brand to gain hands-on experience and expand your knowledge. For example, if you are a personal trainer, you can volunteer to coach a sports team or lead fitness classes at a local community center. These experiences can help you learn new skills and build your brand.

Staying up-to-date on industry trends is crucial to maintaining your personal brand. Follow industry-related news sources, blogs, and social media accounts to stay informed about new developments and trends. Consider subscribing to industry-related publications or conferences to gain further knowledge and insights into your field.

Seeking feedback from others is a great way to improve and refine your brand. Consider asking for feedback from colleagues, mentors, and even clients to gain insights into how others perceive your brand. Use this feedback to continuously make necessary changes and improvements to your personal brand.

Evolving Your Personal Brand as Your Career Grows

Creating a personal brand is an ongoing process that should evolve as your career grows. As you gain more experience, develop new skills, and explore new industries, your personal brand should reflect these changes. This section will discuss ways to ensure that your brand remains relevant and appealing as your career evolves.

Your branding elements, such as your logo, colors, and fonts, are crucial to your personal brand. As your career grows and evolves, revisiting these elements and ensuring they align with your brand and its message is a good idea. You may find that your current branding elements no longer reflect your personality, values, or the image you want to convey to your audience. Consider updating your branding elements to better align with your current professional identity.

As your career evolves, your message may need to be refined to reflect your new experiences and expertise. Reflect on what you've learned, the skills you've gained, and the industries you've explored. Consider how these experiences have changed your perspective and the message you want to convey to your audience. Be intentional with your message and ensure it resonates with your audience while reflecting your professional identity.

A content strategy is an essential aspect of personal branding, and it can help you remain relevant as your career grows. As you develop new skills and expertise, create content that showcases your knowledge and experience. Use social media platforms, blogs, and other relevant channels to share your insights and perspectives with your audience. Developing a consistent content strategy can help you stay top of mind with your audience while building credibility and authority in your industry.

Collaborating with others can be an effective way to expand your network and build your personal brand. Seek opportunities to collaborate with other professionals in your industry or related fields. Collaborations can take various forms, including guest blogging, co-hosting events, or working on a joint project. Collaborating with others can help you gain exposure to new audiences, insights into different industries, and build relationships with other professionals.

Staying engaged with your audience is an essential aspect of personal branding, and it becomes even more critical as your career evolves. Make an effort to respond to comments and messages from your followers and engage with them on social media platforms. Use tools like polls and surveys to gather feedback from your audience and adjust your content strategy accordingly. Building and maintaining a strong relationship with your audience is a critical aspect of personal branding and can help you remain relevant and influential as your career grows.

CONCLUSION

Building a personal brand is crucial in today's world. It helps you stand out from the crowd, establish credibility, and achieve your professional goals. Following the steps outlined in this eBook, you can create a personal brand that truly represents who you are, what you stand for, and what you want to achieve.

Start by identifying your unique value proposition, defining your target audience, and crafting your brand messaging. Develop your brand identity by choosing your branding elements, such as your logo, colors, and fonts. Build your online presence by creating a website, social media profiles, and other platforms showcasing your expertise.

To market and maintain your evolving personal brand, create a marketing plan that includes content creation, influencer marketing, and other tactics that help you reach your target audience. Keep your personal brand up-to-date as your career grows by regularly reassessing your brand messaging, branding elements, and online presence.

Building a personal brand takes time and effort, but the rewards are worth it. With a strong personal brand, you can establish yourself as an authority in your field, attract new opportunities, and achieve your professional goals.

So, take the first step today and start building your personal brand. By following the strategies and tips outlined in this Book, you can create a powerful and impactful personal brand that helps you succeed and make a difference in the world. Good luck on your personal branding journey!

Made in the USA
Middletown, DE
28 May 2023

31605916R00080